CATHAIR N

NO. 37 · 2020

*Journal of **Westport Historical Society***

The editor thanks the following for their assistance in the preparation of this journal,
Dr. John Bradley, Ann Ludden, Brónach Joyce, Sal O'Connor, Gertie Foley.

We also thank our contributors.
Design and Layout by **Shelly Gannon – Eye in the Clock, Westport**
Printed by **MPS - Multi Packaging Solutions, Westport**
HON. EDITOR: AIDEN CLARKE, ROSBEG, WESTPORT, CO. MAYO.

Cover Image Courtesy of the National Library of Ireland.

ISSN 0332-4117

WESTPORT HISTORICAL SOCIETY

CONTENTS

WALTER McNALLY

John Staunton

Early Life
Walter McNally arrived in Westport in 1906 at the age of twenty two with his family, who were returning from Scranton in Pennsylvania in America to settle in Westport.

His father Patrick had emigrated from Knockboy in Kilmeena in the 1870s with his wife Ann (nee Cannon) to Scranton, where their first child Walter was born, followed by two brothers and three sisters. Ann died in 1902 and Patrick remarried, this time to Maria McGreevy, in Cleveland, Ohio. They had three children to add to the family.

In Westport they opened a butcher's shop on Mill Street, close to the fountain where The Clock stands today.

Walter got married to Molly Staunton from James Street in Westport on Christmas Day in 1908. She was the eldest daughter of Myles and Katie Staunton, who both had family background in Kilmeena. He was a handsome man and was said to have winked at her and won her heart as she was passing by on a bicycle.

Soon afterwards they both got on their bicycles and emigrated to America in 1909. (His family emigrated to America for the second time in 1912, this time on the Lusitania). They settled first in Scranton and moved to Warburg in Idaho where they won 180 acres of land in a lottery and he established a meat business. Their first two children, Paddy and Mary, were born there.

They returned to Ireland in 1911 and settled in Clonbur to run a guest house and bar business, which is now owned by the Burke family. Their growing family was enhanced by the births of Hugh (1912), Bernadette (1914) and Angela (1916) in Clonbur.

Musical Life
Walter McNally was always a singer. As a young boy he sang in St. Patrick's Choir in West Scranton. When he was in Westport in his early twenties, he sang in local concerts in Westport Town Hall and was noted for his manly and genial personality and his participation in concert and domestic entertainment. He was a star of Misses' Gallagher Music Group[1] which presented an operetta in the Town Hall, an event which was long remembered by the music lovers of the town.

---

[1] *Agnes and Kathleen Gallagher had a music academy at their home on Bridge Street. Agnes was a leading light in Cumann na mBan during the War of Independence and took the anti treaty side in the Civil War. She was imprisoned in Kilmainham Jail going on hunger strike twice, resulting in her losing her sight.*

Picture from family scrapbook (Sr Helen McGing).

He had no professional training at all but was now successful in getting backing to train under Doctor Vincent O'Brien who was Director of the Palestrina Choir in Dublin and music tutor to James Joyce and John McCormack. O'Brien believed in him and Walter won the Gold Medal at the Feis Ceoil for baritone in 1915. This led to many engagements and a rapid appreciation as an accomplished baritone with stage presence. The family moved from Clonbur to Dublin to engage fully with musical life.

He was encouraged enough by his success in Dublin to form his own opera company in 1918 which mainly performed concert versions of operas. Dr Vincent O'Brien was musical director and conductor and the singers were largely Irish.

The company opened in the Spring of 1918 at the Empire Theatre (later the Olympia) with a week of operas by Wallace and Benedict. The events were successful, but Walter McNally was stricken with influenza and was unable to sing. This was a great personal disappointment for him and for some other members of the cast who were similarly affected.

The company returned to the Empire in June to present Faust by Gounod, The Lily of Killarney by Benedict, The Bohemian Girl by Balfe and Maritana and Lurline by Wallace.

Newspapers reported that people were turned away almost every night and that the season was without exaggeration the most successful local enterprise yet attempted in Ireland. Lurline and Faust were particularly well received by the audiences. In September the company presented a full stage version of Pagliacci by Leoncavallo at the Empire. The critics paid it a lot of attention. One critic wrote that

> "It was a big compliment to actor-manager Mr. Walter McNally that every seat in the auditorium was filled at the first house a quarter of an hour before he came on clad in his motley garb to ring up the curtain. In his singing here, as throughout the night, he gave free play to dramatic gesture. The McNally stamp of quality was over all the work.
>
> The encouraging fact is that grand opera of this intricate character can be done with such excellence by a purely Dublin company."

During this time in Dublin Molly gave birth to their last child Joan, who was later to marry J.P. Roughneen, a businessman in Kiltimagh, and they lived there with their family for many years.

The company stayed together until the Spring of 1920. They played at venues all over the country, in Limerick, Waterford, Wexford, Cork, Sligo, Derry, Dundalk, and Belfast and once in his native Mayo. In Dublin they played at the Empire and also the Theatre Royal. They also gave concerts at Glasgow and other Scottish cities like Dundee where Gigli was God.

The cast was largely made up of Irish singers. Walter McNally and William Lemass sang baritone, Harry O'Dempsey and William Mulcahy sang tenor, Kathleen McCully, Kitty Fagan and Eily Murnaghan sang soprano, Joan Burke and Bridie Moloney sang mezzo soprano, Florrie Ryan sang contralto and Ted Kelly sang bass.

They presented work by Wallace, Benedict and Balfe including the Irish Ring of Maritana, The Lily of Killarney and The Bohemian Girl. They sang an oratorio by Pagliacci and concert versions of Verdi's Traviata, Ernani, and Il Trovatore, and Sullivan's The Prodigal Son.

Walter McNally was equally appreciated for his songs, which audiences called for again and again. Among the favourites were Farewell in the Desert, The Floral Song, Molly Brannigan, The Trumpeter, The Colleen Bawn, Father's Love from Lurline and The Cornish Dance.

When the company opened for a week in Waterford there was limited standing room only in the packed Coliseum. A local newspaper reported that

> "Walter McNally was, of course, the real attraction. He was hardly ever in better voice, and despite the arduous time he is having, he is still gilt edged as ever. His well-measured notes were poured forth as only this famous baritone can do it. No wonder he got a tremendous reception. His first numbers were Farewell in the Desert, The Floral Song, and Molly Brannigan. These, however, are by no means the best of his repertoire and one longed to hear him give some of his favourites that really show him at his best, such as The Trumpeter, The Colleen Bawn and Father's Love from Lurline."

In February 1919 he guested with the JS. O'Brien Choral and Operatic Society for a performance of Faust in Derry, where he scored a personal triumph as Valentine.

In Sligo on one occasion people queued for hours for tickets but were to be disappointed. The Sligo Champion reported that

> "Mr. McNally was, of course, the main attraction of the bill. His pleasing baritone has lost none of its power and sweetness and his singing drew rounds of applause. He was remarkably good in arias from Faust and The Lily of Killarney. Yet we are puzzled why he omitted singing The Colleen Bawn."

A Belfast critic wrote that

> "we have never heard McNally in more effective vein. He excels in the rendering of native melodies, whether plaintive or romantic, and as an operatic artist his appearance and expression count almost as much as his sonorous and expressive vocalism. He is not merely an artist, however, for he is also an organiser with a fine faculty for diagnosing the popular taste".

When he brought the company to Mayo, they had concerts in Ballina, Castlebar and Westport. In Westport they had to wait for the military to vacate the Town Hall to perform for three nights. The Mayo News reported that

> "The spacious concert hall was filled to overflowing. Mr. McNally himself was received with outbursts of applause on his appearance in the parts allotted to him and those outbursts were repeated when, towards the close of the entertainment, he delivered a short speech thanking the people of Westport for their patronage and support. Mr. McNally, in the course of his statement, referred to the fact that the stage on which he then stood was the one on which he first commenced his career as a singer. The whole entertainment was a musical treat such as we never had in Westport before and it does credit to Mr. McNally's organising capacity. When a boy, residing with his parents in Westport, Mr. McNally was very popular at all our local concerts. Since then, Mr. McNally has attained renown as probably the greatest Irish living baritone".

Walter & teacher in Italy. (Scrapbook, Sr Helen McGing).

Walter McNally gave a farewell concert at the Empire Theatre in Dublin in May 1920 to announce his upcoming departure for Italy for further voice-training and to see how Italian opera was managed.

An evening newspaper reported that

> "The warm place this popular artist occupies in the affections of the people was very strikingly demonstrated last night. After his Irish song scene with Miss Eily Murnaghan the pair were recalled again and again. Through the scene, in which several Irish melodies and ballads were strung together in storied form, applause frequently burst forth, only to be hushed lest any part of the music feast should be missed. At the close Mr McNally graciously thanked the audience for their cordial reception".

Italy

Before he left for Italy, his company had an interesting engagement with conductor Vincent O'Brien which was an omen of future events for Walter McNally. O'Brien conducted an orchestra of twenty three players and the Walter McNally opera chorus of forty voices between the showing of films at the La Scala Theatre (later the Capitol cinema), the first of many similar undertakings.

In Italy he received more musical training and set himself to learn Italian, which for a singer was the most important musical language. He met Margaret Burke Sheridan from Castlebar in Naples when she sang her first Madame Butterfly at the San Carlo Opera House, to great applause. This was the start of a long friendship between the two singers.

He was very much at ease in Italy and sang in a number of operas in Naples under the famous conductor Tullio Serafin, who later conducted at the Metropolitan Opera in New York. One report in Italy said that he had the "beautiful softness and the artistic restraint of that great Irish tenor John McCormack" and mentioned the purity of his tone and his rich, rounded singing.

When McNally was back in Dublin in 1922, he arranged a celebrity concert in November at the Theatre Royal for the return of Margaret Burke Sheridan, who had not been home since 1916, but was well acquainted with the torrid national situation. Despite the turbulent background, the concert was the musical event of the year. The diva received a huge welcome back to Dublin, and she told Walter McNally she was more nervous in Dublin than when she appeared at La Scala in Milan. The critics also loved the power and range of her singing and praised her great beauty. They looked forward to seeing her some day in Dublin in her operatic roles. She was overwhelmed by the warmth of the Dublin reception. McNally himself sang a number of songs and ballads at the concert and thought that Sheridan was in outstanding voice.[2]

Soon afterwards they presented Humperdinck's fairy-tale opera Hansel and Gretel at the Theatre Royal, introducing the young soprano Renee Flynn to the public with Joan Burke, William Lemass and Walter McNally.

America
In 1924 Walter McNally went to America with his wife Molly for a series of concert performances. He sang at the annual dinner of The Friendly Sons of Saint Patrick at the Hotel Astor in New York for St. Patrick's Day and started his American concert tour at the Longacre Theatre in New York. He had a supportive audience in Chicago and an enthusiastic Chicago newspaper described him as

> "a broth of a boy who might be mistaken for Jack Dempsey and who is an athlete as well as a songster. Once he was captain of the Westport Gaelic football team, champions of the West of Ireland".

He sang in The Student Prince at the Great Northern Theatre and had an extended run for some months.

He sang Panis Angelicus at the Mass in the Stadium in Philadelphia to celebrate the 150th anniversary of American Independence with a quarter of a million people. The Evening Bulletin of Philadelphia memorably reported:

> "At the Offertory, Walter McNally sang Panis Angelicus. His voice rang over the loudspeakers with such clearness and intense feeling that it gripped the mighty throng like a spell. It was one of the great moments of the Mass".

He sang at the Golden Gate Theatre in San Francisco and at the Capitol Theatre in Scranton, the town where he was born forty years before.

While in America he crossed the Atlantic a few times, once for a big concert at the Theatre Royal in Dublin in 1926. The Independent reported "A Cardinal Welcome Home" for the singer:

> "It is many years since Walter McNally appeared on a Dublin concert platform. In the interval his fame has been broadcast through the Press and the concert halls of America. For us in his homeland he has lost not one whit of his old winning personality. He has the old smile, the magnetism of stage presence so well remembered. By his performance last night, he delighted his already loyal admirers and has recruited hosts of new ones"

---

2 See https://youtu.be/YuquU8z7H8k

The Independent interestingly went on to report on the gracious and musical compliment that the Army School of Music No.1 Band assisted at the concert. The finale was The National Anthem.

"As if by common instinct the audience remained en masse to hear it. At the opening bars the audience rose to their feet and remained standing till the music ceased. The tune played was The Soldiers Song. Thus, for the first time in a public theatre the Free State National Anthem was officially programmed and unanimously and cordially recognised."

Apart from music, he had made many connections in America, including Joe and Rose Kennedy, the parents of the future President. These connections had inspired him with an interest in the cinema business and this was on his mind when he finally returned to live in Dublin.

He had a farewell concert at the Theatre Royal and retired completely from singing at the young age of forty three.

Cinema
He now turned his full attention to the cinema business.

He opened the Savoy Cinema in Galway with John McCormack spinning the first reel. They had both been born in the same year and had remained friends through their singing years.

The cinema venture proved successful and, in the years to come Walter McNally and his family, in association with others at times, opened cinemas in Dublin, Ballina, Athlone, Cork, Wexford and Limerick. He also ran a successful restaurant in Dublin's O'Connell Street. Through these years he took a great interest in the development of young singers and often had musical evenings in the family home, Addison Lodge in Glasnevin, where his wife Molly was a friendly hostess.

Finale
Walter McNally died in 1945 at the age of sixty one. The Evening Mail reported

"Death has rung down the curtain on a colourful career and Dublin has lost a vivid personality in Walter McNally, opera singer turned film distributor. It was a curious decision for an operatic star who had studied in Milan and sang operatic roles in Italy to abandon his musical career at its height and spend the remainder of his life in film renting and cinema ownership. But he proved as successful in business as he had in opera and handled very large interests with the utmost efficiency".

It was a curious coincidence that John McCormack and he shared the same birth year and death year. In another coincidence, he and James Joyce won Feis Ceoil medals and both opened cinemas. Walter McNally's travels from Scranton to Westport, Idaho, Clonbur, Chicago and Italy may not have been as adventurous as those of Ulysses, but they certainly contributed to an interesting life.

All his children are dead now and his grandchildren are mostly in the Dublin area and America, (one in South Africa, one buried in Kiltimagh). Walter's nephew Bill Nealon, who was a federal judge in Scranton and who died in the last year aged ninety-two, was a regular visitor with his family, and he met with the opera buffs in Westport, including the fine tenor Joe McNally, although unrelated, and the late Patsy Staunton, the opera guru. Bill's sister Nancy was another visitor with great stories, and she lives still in Scranton, hale and hearty.

John Staunton lives in Westport and is a nephew of Walter McNally's wife Molly and is a great admirer of Beniamino Gigli. As a child he stayed for a short spell with the McNally family in Addison Lodge in Glasnevin and when he worked as an engineer in New York he and his wife visited Walter's sister Anne Nealon and family in Scranton Pennsylvania.

Main source: Irish Stars of the Opera; Smith (1994). Madison Publishing, Dublin.

Listen at: www.archive.org/details/78_the-exiles-return_walter-mcnally-needham-locke_gbia0069741b

St Patrick's Church, Aughagower photographed at about the turn of the 20th Century.
This was where Margaret Knight & her family were baptised & would have attended weekly Mass.

MARGARET 'MEG' KNIGHT CONNERY: THE WESTPORT SUFFRAGETTE

Mícheál Casey

Margaret 'Meg' Connery, who was born as Margaret Knight near Westport, Co. Mayo in 1881, became a leading figure in the Irish militant suffragette movement of the early twentieth century, and was very prominent in driving the campaign for voting rights for Irish women. While her name featured prominently in contemporary newspaper reports of her many campaigns and court trials, and even though some of her photos (one in particular), and her extensive writings are prominent in histories of the women's franchise campaign, very little is publicly known of her early and later life. And even within the short window between 1912 and 1918 when she was most active in a very turbulent decade of Irish history that she fully engaged in, there are many gaps in her life story. Above all she is almost unknown and unremembered in her native place, and this article aims to partly correct that and remind readers of this journal of her eventful life and her considerable achievements.

The Knights of Triangle

Meg Connery was born Margaret Knight at Mahanagh, Ayle, Aughagower, Westport, Co. Mayo in 1881. While her birth date is registered on the 27th of June 1881, she was baptised as 'Margaret Night' in St Patrick's Catholic Church, Aughagower on 30th April 1881 and her true birth date was probably in the preceding week. Mahanagh remains the official townland name for her native place but it is popularly known as 'Triangle', Ayle. Triangle lies at the junction of the Westport-Ballinrobe road and the side road to Ballyheane about five miles outside Westport. 'Triangle' is an unofficial place-name whose history is at least as ancient as the official 'Mahanagh' and was mentioned in the 7th century 'Tripartite Life of St Patrick' as the location of the 'Well of Stringle', and the ancient pilgrim path to Croagh Patrick, Tóchar Phádraig, passed through the Knight farm.

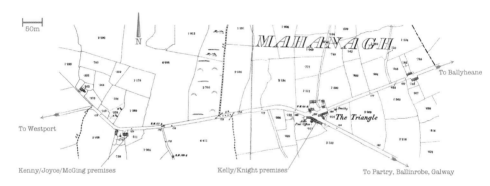

Sketch map adapted by author from 25": 1 mile Ordnance Survey Map, surveyed 1888-1913

Map of Mahanagh/Triangle showing the Knight family's Pub & Post Office

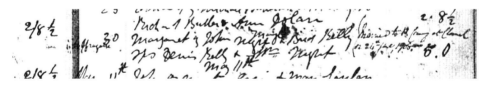

Transcript of April 1881 entry in Baptismal Register of St. Patricks Church Aughagower

Text of Baptismal Record:

(April) 30 – Margaret of John Night & Brid Kelly sps Denis Kelly & Mrs Night.
Later note in right margin: 'Married to P Connery at Clonmel on 24th June 1908.
Later note in left margin: 'Suffragette'.

Registration of Birth of Margaret Knight 1881

At the time Margaret Knight was born, the Knight family were relatively prosperous by the standards of the late 1800s in west Mayo, having a 52-acre farm of good quality limestone land, a public house, and the Ayle post office franchise. The pub where Margaret grew up was informally known as 'The Triangle Parlour' and had been owned by the Kellys, her mother's side of the family. The Westport-Ballinrobe Road was subject to periodic flash-flooding from the Ayle River at this point, locally described by the phrase "Ayle is down". The 'Triangle Parlour' occasionally provided accommodation for stranded travellers heading from Galway to Westport, who had to let the flood waters subside & reveal the road before proceeding west. Margaret's father John C. Knight came from nearby Killawalla and her mother was Bridget Kelly of Triangle/Mahanagh; they were married in Aughagower on the 8th September 1877. The long-established pub business of 'Knight's Parlour' and the location at a prominent crossroads on a busy main road between Westport and Galway suggests that the pub must have been a lively centre of topical discussion, local & wider news, and lively arguments. It is therefore not surprising that Margaret Knight grew up with an interest in national and international matters, especially in a family with an active interest in politics - both her father John C. Knight and her brother Frank Knight were in their turn involved in local activism and politics.

Margaret was the third eldest of nine children born to John Knight of Tawnynagry, Killawalla & Bridget Kelly of Mahanagh - John, Mary, Margaret (later called Meg), Dennis, Bridget (Bridie), Eugene, James (Jim), Francis (Frank), Elizabeth (Lily). Dennis died in infancy aged just 3 months. Bridie Knight's death on the 1st July 1908 aged 14 was reported in that week's Mayo News, but this appears to have been a cruel and unsolved hoax, and a retraction & apology was published in the same paper a week later.

Margaret's brother Frank Knight later joined a local IRA Company during the War of Independence & Civil War, which had robbed a number of post offices. On 16th April 1924, after Irish independence and the end of the Civil War, Margaret & Frank's youngest sister Lily Knight was arrested and charged, by the Postmaster General, with fraudulently handling some stolen postal orders given to her by her brother Frank from the proceeds of a post office robbery. Lily Knight stated that had 'sent these to her brother-in-law in Dublin to settle a debt', presumably referring here to Margaret's husband. In a contemporary letter to Hanna Sheehy-Skeffington, Margaret confided that Lily had done this to 'help the lads on the run' and was quite fearful her youngest sister might get a significant jail term. At a court hearing in Westport on 22nd November 1924, Lily Knight, described as a "very pre-possessing and well-dressed young lady", was discharged under the First Offenders' Act. In his later years, living as a bachelor in a boarding house in Stockport in the UK, Frank was declined an IRA 1916-1921 service medal ('service not established'). It is not clear how these events were related to each other, nor if this episode was the reason for the subsequent transfer of the Ayle post office franchise to the neighbouring pub & grocery business (McGing's) in 1929. Frank Knight is remembered by people now living in the area as a likeable man, self-educated, and a voracious reader but perhaps not the most practical. One neighbour's memory is of him rehearsing political speeches in a mirror before delivering them from a lorry after Mass at Fianna Fáil election rallies in Aughagower village. As an example of Frank Knight's many interests, he was the sole source for all of the local folklore and folk cures for people and farm animals recorded by the local school master Owen Hughes in Knockrooskey National School's contribution to the National Folklore Collection in the 1930s.

The next house to the Knights on the Westport side, which was also a pub (Kenny's, then McGing's, later Digger Jay's) was briefly, in the early 1900s, the home of the family of William Joyce. William was later to gain infamy during World War 2 as the Nazi propagandist Lord Haw-Haw who broadcast a fascist radio propaganda show known as "Germany Calling" into the UK & Ireland, from Nazi Germany throughout the war. He was shot & captured at the end of the war and was executed by Britain as an alleged traitor to his British passport in 1946. It seems likely Margaret Knight would have known the young William Joyce & his family as next door neighbours when he was a young child.[1]

The Knight home and farm holding were sold at auction in the 1950s and the remains of the original house & its associated outbuildings were demolished in living memory (1980s) in road widening operations to improve the safety for traffic of what was a dangerous junction on a bend.

Margaret's father John C. Knight was deeply involved in the local nationalist & land ownership movements of the turn of the 20th century and was the President of the local parish (Aughagower) branch of the United Irish League. The "cattle drive" movement emerged in the early 1900s, when bullocks were driven off a contested farm holding as a form of protest. The slogan that accompanied this movement was "the road for the bullocks & the land for the people!". John C. Knight led one

---

1 *William Joyce's cradle can be seen in the Clew Bay Heritage Centre, Westport(Ed.).*

The Capture of William Joyce, 'Lord Haw Haw', northern Germany, 1945.
This notorious Nazi propagandist and broadcaster was briefly (as an infant) a next door neighbour of the Knight family in Ayle, when his father bought a pub there before the Joyces moved to Galway and thence to England after Independence. This photo shows William Joyce lying in an ambulance under armed guard before being taken from British 2nd Army Headquarters to hospital. He had been shot in the thigh at the time of his arrest.

such cattle drive on the 12th Dec 1911 when a crowd of about a thousand people gathered in Aughagower and drove all 120 of the cattle from Lord Sligo's farm in Teevenish, beside Aughagower, to the landlord's rent office on Castlebar Street, Westport (opposite the Court House, where the Castlecourt Hotel stands now). John C. Knight led the action and at its conclusion he managed a peaceful dispersal of the crowd during a potentially explosive stand-off with the armed police of the Royal Irish Constabulary on Castlebar Street. He was among a number of men, who were subsequently charged with public order offences, but the charges seem to have been quietly dropped at around the time the land was divided among the tenants. John C. Knight was a veteran of land agitation having been the proposer of the motion to form a parish branch of the Land League in Aughagower more than thirty years earlier in 1880. The cattle drive was ultimately successful in its twin aims which were to force Lord Sligo to reduce his rent and to sell the land to the local tenants through the Congested Districts Board.

REGISTER OF Ballyburke NATIONAL SCHOOL

Date of Entrance, 1902	Register Number	Pupils' Names in Full	Age of Pupil last Birth Day	Religious Denomination	Residence	Occupation or Means of Living of Parents	School	County	Class
June 30th	272 ¹	Leonard S. Basquill	7	R.C.	Kelladee +	Accountant	Roundstone	Galway	1st
Jan. 1st	244 ²	Jas. Murphy	7	R.C.	Ballyburke	Farmer	Trans from Infts		2nd
" "	253 ³	Thos. Benedict Lyons	6	R.C.	Kelladee	"	"	"	"
" "	254 ⁴	Jos. Kirby	7	R.C.	Ballyburke	"	"	"	"
" "	260 ⁵	Frank Knight	6	R.C.	Agle (Triangle)	"	"	"	"

Photo by Mary Gavin 2019
Although Margaret Knight's primary school educational records have not been discovered to date the records of five of her siblings attending Ballyburke National School suggest she must have also gone there – this is the enrolment record of her younger brother Frank. The records for the older girls Margaret (Meg), Mary (Mollie) and Bridget (Bridie) are missing, presumably all in the same, now lost, Girls' Roll Book.

A varied education and employment

While Margaret Knight's family were relatively prosperous compared to many of their neighbours, as the third eldest from a family of nine children, there certainly would not have been the means to procure a secondary education for Margaret and her siblings in Ireland at the time. The fees and the need to forego a teenager's farm labour or earning capacity put secondary education beyond ordinary farming families. These were hard times in west Mayo, and a minor famine (An Gorta Beag) had occurred in 1879, just two years before Margaret Knight's birth. Margaret would have gone to school in her local primary school like her siblings, probably in Ballyburke National School. Only fragmentary Ballyburke NS records survive confirming that several of the Knight children were enrolled. Most Irish primary school pupils left school & any further contact with education forever at the age 12 or 13 in that era.

In an unusual turn of events for the period, just after Margaret left primary school in Ballyburke, the entire Knight family emigrated to New York on the 'Campania' from Queenstown (Cobh), Co. Cork, on the 3rd June 1894, arriving at Ellis Island, New York six days later. One fortunate effect of this adventure seems to have been a slight extension of Margaret's formal education, and in her later years she recalled that she was very happy in school in New York and that she had been reluctant to return to Ireland as a result. In an even more unusual development, most of the emigrant Knight family returned home within a few years of their joint departure. It has not so far been possible to identify exactly when the family returned home, but Mrs Knight and her eight children are recorded back in their home in Triangle on the 1901 Census, and her husband John C. Knight is back in the family home in the 1911 census. Again, it was even more unusual for an entire family to return to Ireland from America, than it was for an entire & large family to emigrate together. This early travel is likely to have been a formative experience in broadening Margaret Knight's outlook and experience.

In spending the rest of her life in Ireland, Margaret Knight differed from her siblings, who all seem to have eventually emigrated (including even her brother Frank who inherited the family farm). We have limited information about her family life, except snippets in letters she wrote later in her life. She recalls in her sixties that she never felt she was favoured by her mother, but that she had an uncle (Fr J.J. Kelly) who was a Franciscan priest in Clonmel Friary in Co. Tipperary, who mentored and encouraged her. In particular, he nurtured the young Margaret's interest in reading, by providing her with a steady supply of well-selected books. He was himself a published novelist and clearly heavily influenced her literary development, and she became a very fine writer and orator. At some point after Margaret returned from America with her mother and siblings, she moved to live in Clonmel, where her informal but structured self-education continued, and she also enrolled in classes where she learned shorthand and typing. From Clonmel, she moved to Dublin where she obtained employment as a shorthand-typist with a printing firm. In an early rehearsal of her later political phase, she used her forceful negotiating skills to rapidly bargain her salary upwards. She is also recorded as having worked as a drapery assistant in Arnott's department store in this period. With trade union activist and feminist Cissie Cahalan, she became involved in the Irish Women Workers' Union. Margaret continued to build relentlessly on her educational foundation all through her life as a voracious reader of newspapers, magazines, and books. Many of her letters contain acknowledgements & requests for reading material, or her own pithy reviews of works recently read. She had a particular taste for the political and left-wing literature and her socialist and feminist principles heavily influenced her reading selection and tastes: books about Russia are mentioned, as well as books made available through the socialist 'Left Book Club'.

John (Jarlath) Kelly   **(1851-1873-1924)**

John was a Mayoman from Ballinrobe who became Jarlath when he went to the novitiate in Drogheda in 1872. He studied in Rome and was ordained in 1876. He taught in St. Francis Academy, Clonmel, 1879-81, and also became known as a novelist. He wrote a fictional life of St. John Nepomucene. Jarlath was superior in Thurles 1881-82 and then moved to Limerick. He went to Carrick-on-Suir in 1887, changing to Clonmel in 1889. He moved to Galway in 1895, returning to Clonmel in 1901. He went to Waterford in 1918. Jarlath went to meet the Lord in the friary and was buried, as the custom then was, in the friary graveyard in Carrick-on-Suir.

Unpublished biographical note on Margaret Knight's uncle, Father Jarlath (John) Kelly, extracted from internal Franciscan records & kindly supplied by Father Larry Mulligan, Franciscan Friary, Clonmel. Putting his place of birth as 'Ballinrobe' is an understandable error, as he was from 'Ballinrobe Road, Westport'

Marriage and life in Dublin

Margaret Knight married John Patrick 'Con' Connery, a Limerick man, in Clonmel, Co Tipperary in 1909. It is presumed that she met him in the capital, for they both had Dublin addresses when they were married by her Franciscan uncle Fr J.J. Kelly in the Franciscan Friary, Clonmel on the 20th July 1909. Con Connery gives his occupation as clerk in their marriage records, and later in his career he was a Civil Service executive officer, with a position in the Board of Works (now known as the Office of Public Works), headquartered at St. Stephens Green in Dublin. Both of the Connerys are absent from the 1911 Census of Ireland, which the Irish suffragette movement largely boycotted as a protest. Clearly, they believed that if they didn't count for voting, they would not be counted in the Census!

Con & Margaret (by now known as Meg) Connery initially lived in 24 Kildare St, Dublin 2, opposite Leinster House, and just around the corner from Con's workplace, and presumably convenient to Meg's own employment. Later in her life, she & Con moved out to the southern suburbs of the city and, given their frequent changes of address around Rathmines and Rathgar throughout their lives, it seems likely that they continued to rent rather than purchase. They appear to have had a very happy marriage, which was marred by a miscarriage in 1914, which took a very severe mental and physical toll on Meg. She does not appear to have had any more children, and the remainder of her life was regularly blighted by ill-health; regular mentions of periodic episodes of fatigue & depression and frail health feature throughout her correspondence.

Early adventures in political activism

Margaret Knight, now Meg Connery, had embarked on activities associated with her career of radical militant activism from her base in Dublin within two years of her marriage: She had evidently become involved in the campaign for voting rights for women and 'radicalised' in the more militant (for the time) tactics of the Irish suffragette movement that she adopted shortly after her arrival in Dublin. Meg Connery and many of the other household names who became active in the campaign for women's voting equality lived in the southern Dublin suburbs of Rathgar, Rathmines, Ranelagh, Donnybrook and Sandymount, and knew each other socially. Hanna Sheehy Skeffington and Margaret Cousins had set up a new suffrage group in Dublin in 1908, named the Irish Women's Franchise League (IWFL). This group was impatient for change and ready to challenge social conventions. Although women-only, men could be associate members and two of the early male associates were the husbands of the founding members – Francis Sheehy Skeffington and James Cousins. While there is no record of how they met, Meg's acquaintance with Hanna Sheehy Skeffington grew into a deep and life-long friendship as well as suffragette comradeship. Meg joined the IWFL in the spring of 1909, and rose rapidly within the young organisation, and was chairing a

Margaret (Meg) Connery. A scan of an original image in the Loretta Clarke Murray Collection Margaret (Meg) Connery nee Knight – portrait photo by Stanley Photo Studios, Dublin, autographed in Irish script by the subject as Maigréad Ní Connaire. Date unknown, but probably shortly after her marriage in 1909.

meeting of the IWFL in Dublin in their headquarters on 24th October 1911, a month before her father led the famous Teevenish cattle drive at home in Westport. She soon became vice-Chairwoman of the IWFL.

By 1911 the Home Rule campaign had gained momentum, and the IWFL was building up pressure for the emerging momentum for Home Rule to incorporate a measure of self-determination for Irish women as well as Irish men. At the meeting on 24 Oct 1911, Meg declared that they were not going to have this question put back, and if it was not settled, they would treat the Irish Members of Parliament "the same way the Englishwomen treated Asquith". She was referring to the English

Mrs. Sheehy-Skeffington (in widow's weeds) with the banner of Irish Women's Franchise League.

Photo of Meg Connery (R) and Hanna Sheehy-Skeffington (L) with the new IWFL Banner 1916.

suffragette campaign of breaking windows in government buildings and the homes of politicians, including that of Prime Minister HH Asquith, and giving a strong hint of the next steps in the Irish suffragette campaign.

A month later, Meg was among 131 militant suffragettes arrested on Tuesday 21 November 1911 for breaking windows in government buildings in Parliament Square and in the Strand in London. This was a co-ordinated day of action when suffragettes produced concealed hammers and smashed windows across central London. Meg broke windows in the War Office at the junction of Horse Guards Parade and the Strand. Like the others, Meg Connery was convicted in a London court and fined 10 shillings with 10 shillings damages or seven days imprisonment in default of payment.

Like many others, she refused to pay the fine, so she was jailed in Holloway Prison. An Irish Times report of the hearing said, "Mrs Connery said that Irish women were prepared to resist any government, Home Rule or otherwise, that did not recognise them". The imprisoned Irish women were released at the end of their terms and returned to a hero's welcome in Dublin on 5 Dec 1911.

In February 1912, Meg Connery & three colleagues from the IWFL including Hanna Sheehy Skeffington heckled and interrupted Winston Churchill, then First Lord of the Admiralty, and later Prime Minister, mid-speech at a large public meeting on Home Rule in Celtic Park, Belfast. The women shouted "Will the Liberal government give Home Rule to Irish women? We demand votes for women under the Home Rule Bill!". Along with the other suffragettes who heckled Churchill, Meg Connery was forcibly & roughly ejected from the meeting.

In all her suffragette activities, Meg was closely allied with her close friend Hanna Sheehy Skeffington, whose husband Francis was notoriously taken prisoner by the British Army when Dublin was under Martial Law in the immediate aftermath of the 1916 Rising. Francis Skeffington was a Cavan-born pacifist and a feminist, far ahead of

Connery, Mrs Margaret	Breaking window War Office	10. 0	7 days 2nd Div.	10/-

Charge details & sentence handed down in case of Meg Connery at Bow St Magistrate's Court in London, copied from the UK Home Office's Records. Meg was arrested, tried, and sentenced for breaking windows in HM War Office on Wednesday 23rd November 1911.

his time, and at the time of his marriage to the Irish Parliamentary Party MP's daughter Hanna Sheehy they both combined their surnames to emphasise the equality of their partnership. Francis Sheehy Skeffington was arrested by British soldiers while trying to stop looting in Dublin in the aftermath of the 1916 Easter Rising, who briefly used him as a hostage/human shield, and then summarily executed him, with two other equally innocent journalists, without even the pretence of a trial, on the direct order of Captain J.C. Bowen-Colthurst. This occurred in Portobello Barracks on 26 April 1916. Even by the standards of a period with many outrages, and even under the sweeping powers of Martial Law, this was widely regarded as a cold-blooded murder. Meg Connery supported her widowed friend Hanna through this period and accompanied her to the Court Martial that followed in Richmond Barracks, which found Bowen-Colthurst guilty but insane. The general public disappointment with this verdict turned to outrage when Bowen-Colthurst was released after just a year in Broadmoor Mental Hospital, and eventually allowed to emigrate to Canada. Hanna Sheehy Skeffington added her personal campaign to clear her late husband's name, and her pursuit of justice on his behalf, to her already very active suffragette and nationalist campaigning.

Life in the spotlight

Meg Connery was a physically small person, and when she was imprisoned for yet more window-breaking, this time in Dublin in 1913, her height was recorded in the Tullamore Prison register with Edwardian exactitude as 5' 01/2".Her relatively low stature was accentuated in some surviving photos where she was pictured beside the 6'2" Madame Maud Gonne McBride Despite her diminutive size, she was recalled by those who knew her as a dynamic bundle of energy, razor sharp and direct in her debating style.

In their joint autobiography "We Two Together" the activist couple James & Margaret Cousins remember Meg's lively engagement in the rough and tumble days of open political meetings as follows:

> "The memory of Meg Connery comes up, short, spare, taut, one foot on the upturned edge of the lorry, head thrown back, eyes shining, as she parries thrusts, thrusts back, gets a cheer for a palpable hit, and, not being of the kind that is satisfied with the plaudits of the ignorant or vulgar, lets out with a lash that looks like stirring anger in the crowd."

Library of Congress Left-Right: Meg Connery, Mary Kettle, Kate Sheehy and Hanna Sheehy Skeffington arriving for the court martial of Captain Bowen Colthurst at Richmond Barracks, Inchicore for the murder of Hanna's husband Francis Sheehy Skeffington on 6th June 1916. Image Courtesy of the National Library of Ireland.

Several examples of Meg Connery's rapid rhetorical responses are preserved in contemporary accounts, such as on 11 May 1915, a year before the Easter Rising, when Meg chaired a meeting of the Irish Women's Franchise League at the Trades' Hall in Dublin city centre, held to protest at the exclusion of any Irish delegate from attending the International Women's Conference at the Hague called to discuss the First World War. A letter to the League, from Padraig Pearse, a year before he led the 1916 Rising, and at that time the headmaster of St Enda's school in Rathfarnham, was read out where he said:

'The action of the British Government in preventing Irish women from attending the Women's International Peace conference is only the latest manifestation of the settled policy of Great Britain to eliminate Ireland from the counsels of Europe and the world. We have now been almost completely cut off from communications with other countries and peoples except through Britain... The present incident will do good if it ranges more of the women definitely with the national forces.'

The last sentence of Pearse's letter above drew an immediate rebuke from Meg Connery as chair of the meeting, recorded as:

'That was a very masculine inversion. The incident ought to have the effect of ranging the national forces on the side of the women (Applause).'

This political and militant activist phase of Meg Connery's life is very well known and publicly documented in the newspapers of the time, so there is only space here for a brief summary of the main points in these action-packed and turbulent years (see bibliography).

The Tullamore Mice (L-R) Meg Connery, Mabel Purser, Margaret Cousins and Barbara Hoskins photographed in Tullamore Prison 1913, while they were serving their sentences for breaking windows in Dublin in protest at yet another setback in the campaign for voting equality for women. Image Courtesy of the National Library of Ireland.

In 1913 Meg Connery and three others again broke windows in Dublin in an act of protest, this time in the Customs House, & she was imprisoned with three other suffragettes in Tullamore, where they achieved national fame as the 'Tullamore Mice'. This nickname came from the 'Cat & Mouse' Bill, a devious piece of British legislation under whose terms suffragette hunger strikers would be released as fasting took its toll, and re-arrested when they regained their strength, toying with them like a cat playing with a mouse. The high media profile of the 'Tullamore Mice' ensured they got exceptionally generous treatment in prison, with fresh cut flowers & extra bedding in their cells, and seemingly unlimited visitors. They were even allowed to take the famous photograph of the 'Tullamore Mice' which survives in the collection of the National Library of Ireland.

Meg did not forget her western roots, and along with Hanna Sheehy-Skeffington, she tackled the challenge of a gap in suffragette support in Connaught with a series of meetings that included dates in her hometown (Westport Town Hall), in Longford, and in Boyle Co. Roscommon. In these venues their unpopular message in a traditional society attracted vitriolic hostility, jeering and jostling which often threatened to boil over into rioting.

The Irish Independent of 7th March 1914 gives a flavour of the intimidation they faced down in Boyle and the risks they took for their cause:

SUFFRAGETTE RIOT IN BOYLE
Mrs Sheehy Skeffington & Mrs Connery addressed a suffragette meeting in Boyle on Thursday night, the eve of the March fair, with the result that the hall in which they spoke was attacked by a crowd, and windows broken, while rotten eggs were thrown in at the doors. The police dispersed the crowd in front of the hall by a baton charge and volley of bottles and stones were thrown at the police from laneways. The ladies were escorted to their hotel by over 20 police being loudly hooted as they proceeded. The hotel windows were broken, and on the police again charging, the windows of shops and private houses were smashed. The hotel was guarded for the night.

An almost equally boisterous & hostile reception ensued in Westport Town Hall on the night of Friday 24th January 1913, when Meg and Margaret Cousins addressed a similar meeting. The newspapers noted that there had been 'disorder, heckling and general rowdyism', with the Mayo News stating that the proceedings were 'unique in the history of public meetings in Westport'. However, the IWDL deemed these events a success because of the profile achieved for the cause, the demand for literature, and the recruitment of members to the League that followed.

Meg with Carson & Bonar Law
The most well-known image of Meg Connery, confronting Andrew Bonar Law (left) and Edward Carson (right), as a Dublin Metropolitan Police constable dashes behind Carson to detain Meg. This image captures the pugnacity & fearless audacity of both Meg & the campaign of the IWFL. Out of shot, Hanna Sheehy Skeffington was making a similar protest but unlike Meg she was arrested and charged with assaulting a policeman. Meg Connery was briefly detained and released without arrest. Image Courtesy of the National Library of Ireland.

The Irish Citizen was a newspaper established largely to promote the IWFL and the campaign for voting equality, and Meg Connery was a prolific contributor throughout its existence from its foundation in 1912 till its Dublin printing presses were smashed by the Black & Tans in 1921. Meg Connery's articles in the Irish Citizen were lively, well-argued and erudite, and reveal a sharp mind, and a sophisticated mastery of the English language & the art of rhetoric. Most were by-lined with her name, but some of the more contentious articles on aspects of public and private morality attributed to her are credited as 'by M.K.C.' (Margaret Knight Connery).

The event she is most remembered for nowadays occurred in November 1913, when she interrupted a photo-call by the leading Dublin unionist & barrister (later politician) Edward Carson and the then leader of the Conservative Party (& later Prime Minister of Great Britain), Andrew Bonar Law. They had been attending a meeting of the British Conservative Party in Dublin, after which Bonar Law &

Carson had lunch with Lord Iveagh in Iveagh House on St Stephen's Green (now the headquarters of the Department of Foreign Affairs). When leaving Iveagh House, the dignitaries paused on the front steps for photos. The ever-alert suffragettes saw their chance and pounced - a photo of Meg Connery stepping between the two men and thrusting a bundle of suffragette literature in Bonar Law's direction has become an iconic image of the Irish militant suffragette movement, and a symbol of their campaign. It has been used in numerous publications and websites, especially those covering the centenary of the first votes for women in 1918. Most recently it has featured on the covers of both Louise Ryan's recent book 'Winning the vote for women' and the 2018 catalogue of the Four Courts Press. Hanna Sheehy Skeffington & Meg Connery were detained on the spot by the Dublin Metropolitan Police, with Hanna arrested and charged with assaulting a policeman, who she accused of injuring her. Although the photo shows the constable rushing in to detain Meg, she was not arrested on this occasion..

After women were granted the vote in 1918 (albeit in a very restricted manner, but on equal terms to men), Meg Connery continued to campaign for other rights for women and directed her attention to aspects of the fight for Irish independence and in particular pursuing the human rights abuses committed by the Black & Tans in Munster. With the British feminist & suffragette Emmeline Pethick-Lawrence, Meg Connery spent a period in Cork, Tipperary, & Limerick in 1921 with the White Cross organisation compiling a comprehensive report consisting of personal accounts of the indignities and sexual assaults committed on Irish women by the Black & Tans.

Meg Connery also fundraised for the relief of suffering in Ireland caused by the War of Independence and for the rights of prisoners, especially those who remained imprisoned in England after the end of the Civil War, when her sympathies remained firmly with the Republican side.

In 1923 Meg spent a holiday in Eccles' Hotel, Glengarriff, Co. Cork for the express purpose of meeting & lobbying the playwright George Bernard Shaw to use his influence to gain the release of republican prisoners from British prisons. She met Shaw on several occasions in Cork, and later at his home in London, and ultimately convinced him to write an open letter in support of granting political status to the republican prisoners to the Manchester Guardian (now The Guardian) on 24 Oct 1924.

In the 1920s and again in the 1930s Meg Connery travelled through England and America as a Sinn Féin activist, speaking publicly, lobbying and fund-raising alongside Charlotte Despard. She supported Fianna Fáil when it split from Sinn Féin but she ultimately became disenchanted with what she viewed as De Valera's 'despicable' attitude to women & mocked his religious piety, eventually declaring that she wished he would "retire to some monastery where he could spend the rest of his days telling his beads!"

We know that in 1925 Meg Connery was in America, where she posed for a striking photograph with the legendary American suffragette and women's rights activist Alice Paul. In a sad twist the date of this particular photograph (3rd December 1925) probably explains Meg's absence from her father's funeral at home in Mayo. John C. Knight died on the 26th November 1925 and was buried on the following day in Aughagower graveyard. Meg Connery was conspicuous by her absence from the published account of her father's funeral, but she was represented in her absence from the country by her husband, Con Connery.

An interview with Meg from this trip with a syndicated American journalist, George Britt, was widely published in American regional newspapers. This quirky piece gave a flavour of her radical ideas, where Meg Connery argued for the liberation of women from kitchen duties, and for the creation of community kitchens to that end. Her reasoning was that it was no more a woman's role to cook for the family than it was the man's role to repair their shoes! She reasoned if shoe repair could be professionalised on a community basis, then so could other menial work like cooking.

In the late 1920s and early 1930s Meg fundraised for the Irish republican cause, but she was deeply frustrated by the way the splintering of the movement at home undermined the coherence of the message she was tasked with disseminating in North America.

Meg's politics continued to drift to the left as she became disillusioned with the emerging Irish Free State, with De Valera, and the role of the church. In 1930 she went on a tour of Russia with fellow feminist Rosamond Jacob as the sole Irish representatives of the 'Irish Friends of Soviet Russia', a journey which is chronicled in great detail in Rosamond's diaries.

Fading from view...

From the mid-1930s, Meg Connery's public profile and her political activism gradually faded out. Her later life was occupied with close contact with her former fellow campaigners & lifelong friends in 'retirement from active service', many of whom lived in the Ranelagh/Rathmines/Rathgar area of south Dublin. Her letters from this era record a wide and active social circle, and a genteel and comfortable lifestyle, being invited to tea, and returning the compliment. In particular Meg enjoyed weekend walks with her husband Con & her friends. A group of pals, including Hanna Sheehy Skeffington, Cissie Cahalan, and others associated with

Fancy Dress group L-R Meg Connery Hannah Sheehy Skeffington, Margaret Cousins and Con Connery at an IWFL fancy dress event. Undated photo from the Sheehy Skeffington Collection in the National Library of Ireland. There was an IWFL fund-raiser in 1917 and this is a possible date for this photo. Photo in Sheehy Skeffington Collection in the National Library of Ireland. Image Courtesy of the National Library of Ireland.

the IWFL, who called themselves 'the Pilgrims', met regularly for Sunday walks and lively discussions of socialist politics in the foothills of the Dublin Mountains. A typical itinerary was a tram trip from Harcourt Street or Ranelagh to Carrickmines, from where they walked to the Scalp, & onwards to lunch in Enniskerry.

There is a clear impression from what survives of Meg Connery's correspondence that she deeply missed the cut and thrust of her activist years in later life and missed her life on the front line. In particular her letters to Hanna Sheehy Skeffington, and her later letters to Hanna's son Owen Sheehy Skeffington after Hanna's death, show that she was frustrated by the failure of her later life to regain the tempo and intensity of the 'revolutionary decade' whose centenary we continue to mark. Meg was utterly devastated by the death of her beloved husband Con Connery, who died from bowel cancer and cardiac failure in the City of Dublin Hospital on Baggot Street on the 24th June 1950 after a long illness. His published funeral notice stated, 'house private & funeral private' and was in accordance with Meg's belief that funerals were private and morbid occasions that ought to be held in private or as she put it, 'in camera'. Meg suffered a severe nervous breakdown after Con's death, after which she was hospitalised, and she seems to have spent the remaining eight years of her life in institutional care.

Con Connery's death marked the start of a downward spiral in Meg's health, her finances and her most precious attribute, her independence. She remained in residential care throughout her seventies in a series of nursing homes, right through the 1950s, despite ever more frantic attempts by her to secure a pension arising from what she called her 'National Work' in the 1916-1921 period, which appears to have been a fruitless struggle to have her involvement in supporting the fight for independence formally recognised. She believed a pension would buy her freedom from the nursing home and, above all, the nuns she despised. Meg placed great faith in the renowned former Lord Mayor of Dublin Alderman 'Alfie' Byrne to lobby for her, but even he seems to have failed to secure a pension for Meg. In this era, the nature of the covert service people were claiming to have performed meant that it was not always well documented.

Despite the pension disappointments, Meg Connery's fighting spirit remained defiant and in her correspondence she offered regular critiques of the nursing staff, and in particular the nuns, to whom she had a very strong aversion. Her sharp eloquence was now deployed to convey her misery at being confined with people she was not fond of. Her profound grief at the loss of Con was compounded by the loss of her Siamese cat Jasper, who had to be rehomed with the Sheehy Skeffington family in Rathmines as the nursing home would not or could not accommodate him. A sample of her dispatches from these dark days at the end of her life gives a flavour of her sharp pen:

> "It is a bit of a wrench to give up Jasper, the only thing I have left to love, but one has to recognise facts, and my life is bounded by this dismal tenement, where nobody trusts anybody else, and all go in fear of the Jezebel at the top. There is a false gaiety now and then, when somebody bangs the piano, even then there is a rivalry between two performers, and so the pitiful play is played out. This "monotonous regiment of women", with nothing to do, what a waste of common faculties! I used to love living vividly, movement, and colour, and action, and it is the very irony of life that I should find myself at this Dead End! How I envy Con who has escaped to Freedom!"

Meg Connery's sharp wit wasn't confined to her letters: when one nun approached her in one of the residential homes to ask if she had been baptised, Meg replied that she didn't know as she had been too young at the time to remember! However, despite her spirited resistance, the decline in her personal circumstances continued relentlessly.

One particularly poignant letter to Hanna Sheehy Skeffington's son Owen is preserved in the National Library of Ireland. It is written on a small bundle of improvised writing material (several plain postcards, a scrap of cardboard, and a square torn off the bottom of a receipt). She opens the letter stating by way of explanation that this is the only writing paper she can get her hands on. It is undated but can be safely assigned to the early fifties by her reference in the notes to it being 'almost forty years' since the infamous 1913 photo of Meg with Carson & Bonar Law. In fact, she is mainly writing to ask Owen to come in and collect that now-famous photo which was 'shoved behind the press in this room, gathering dust', and she is afraid the nuns will dump it 'in the discards'. Considering how famous & iconic an image it has since become of the Irish suffragette struggle, it is astonishing to think how close it came to being lost forever. In the years that followed, Meg Connery continued in residential care in a series of institutional residential settings, each of which in their turn disappointed her.

Margaret (Meg) Knight Connery died of 'myocardial degeneration' (heart failure) in St Brendan's Hospital, Grangegorman on the 6th December 1958, and her official death record records her as 'of no fixed address'. No record of her place of burial has been discovered at the time of publication.

The small and fearless woman from Ayle who fought so heroically and articulately for the equal place of women in Irish society ended her days with no place of her own.

Acknowledgements
Firstly, thanks to Aiden Clarke, editor of 'Cathair na Mart', who I am embarrassed to admit first brought the existence of Meg Connery to my attention (literally a 'neighbour's child' to my ancestors) and suggested this article last year. I am very grateful to Micheline Sheehy Skeffington for her family anecdotes and key leads, and to Dr Margaret Ward for her warm encouragement and information on Meg Connery's role in the suffrage movement, and to both ladies for their friendly & generous support of this project. This article could not have been completed without the ever-helpful staff of the National Library of Ireland and the National Archives, and their meticulously curated documentation. I am also grateful to neighbours

including Sean McGing of Ayle, John-Jo McTigue of Westport and Pat Carney of Teevenish who provided and confirmed crucial details – Pat was the only person I spoke to who personally remembered seeing Meg Connery on her holidays at home in Ayle when he was a small child growing up there. Theresa Hoban NT and her friend Mary Gavin were instrumental in confirming Meg Connery's primary school attendance in the long-closed Ballyburke National School.

Finally, sincere thanks to my wife Karen and my family for their patience with all the time I have spent on this project over the past year, for their continued support, and their helpful comments on the manuscript.

Mícheál Casey is a native of Aughagower, Westport, Co. Mayo. He graduated from UCD's Veterinary College in Ballsbridge in 1989 and worked as a lecturer in veterinary parasitology there for three years before leaving to spend a spell in farm animal veterinary practice in his native Mayo. In 1997 he joined the Regional Veterinary Laboratory in Sligo as a veterinary research officer, becoming officer-in charge in 2004. He graduated with an MSc from the University of London in 2004. He became Head of Regional Veterinary Laboratories based at the Central Veterinary Research Laboratory in Backweston in 2010. He is an adjunct Associate Professor of Veterinary Medicine in UCD. He has had a lifelong interest in local and family history, which has been greatly increased in recent years by the vast amount of original source material & original documentation coming available online. He is married to Karen Moriarty, with a son and three daughters and lives on a smallholding in Tubbercurry Co. Sligo, where he keeps a few Dexter cattle. He has also published Head Constable Richard Scott (1810 – 1865) of Tuam in The Journal of the Old Tuam Society (published November 2018).

WESTPORT'S PRESBYTERIAN CHURCH AND ITS CONGREGATION

Noelene Beckett Crowe

To the residents of Westport at this present time there is no visible existence of the Church or Graveyard within the town. The intention is to hopefully inform citizens of that ministry and its community.

Presbyterians have a faith that has at its core the Discipline evolved from the teachings of John Calvin, (1509 – 1564) and also John Knox 15(15 -1572).[1] The Presbyterian belief was that they as individuals had a covenant with God and expected that their religion and agreements concerning it would be the subject of mutual agreement or covenant.[2]

History

Presbyterianism was brought to Ireland by Scottish Immigrants during 1610 with the plantation of Ulster by King James I. By 1660 over 100,000 Presbyterian members had set up churches or communities in Ireland. The situation was difficult for the newcomers as they were resented by Irish Catholics plus the English Governments policies toward them were inconsistent. Policy changes under James I reign led to the formation of congregations outside of the established Church of Ireland – Anglican Church. One can read in 'The History of the Irish (Presbyterian) Church from the Reformation to the Great Revival of 1625' by Rev. J. G. Graighead that the 1610 Colonization of Ulster brought into effect by Sir Arthur Chichester, Lord – Deputy of the Kingdom to whom was conferred a large estate then acted as an agent. His first act was a careful survey of all the forfeited lands. He drew up a plan for settlements which were allotted to three classes namely; voluntary emigrants from England and Scotland, servants of the Crown then finally natives. Special care was entrusted to the King for the support of the Church. He restored all the Sees to their ecclesiastical positions, parochial churches were reopened, glebes allotted to ministers plus a free school was established in each town within the Diocese. 'A Confession of Faith' was entrusted to Dr. James Usher DD in the College of Dublin.[3] During the 1641 Rebellion against the English by Irish Catholics many thousands of Protestants were murdered. King WilliamIII granted Presbyterians partial toleration but it was 1869 before complete toleration was provided, in the meantime many thousands had emigrated to North America. There were various groups or sects over time i.e.; Covenanters of 1638, Seceders in 1691, Burghers and Anti –

---

1 *Mayo History & Society' (2015); Moran, Gerard & Ó Muraile, Nolláig.*
2 *http://www.ulsternationalist.freeservers.com/custom.html*
3 *https://www.libraryireland.com/ScotchIrishSeeds/VI-4.php*

Burgers, New Light, Old Light then during 1752 the Relief Church was formed.[4] During 1782 marriages performed by ministers were legalized. They were required to keep Registers of baptisms and marriages from 1819. The Marriage Act of 1844 legalized marriages between members of Presbyterians with Church of Ireland community.[5] An edited version of an article was published in the Presbyterian Herald October 2015 by the Deputy Clerk of the General Assembly Jim Stothers (1981) with a question; An lahhrann tú Gailge? Rev. Dr. Henry Cooke appealed for Scots –Irish – speaking ministers to come to Ireland. He possessed an ability to read and speak the language also Cooke desired to evangelize in Irish. Jeremiah O'Quin was the first missionary to provide Irish services in Connacht during 1654.[6]

The main Presbyterian body was formed by the Synod of Munster that included Dublin, West and South Ireland with the Synod of Ulster responsible for those within the six counties. Eventually the various groups united. Several doctrinal controversies occurred among congregations during the eighteen and nineteenth centuries with the result that a small group formed a Unitarian faction. During the mid – twenty century the Irish Presbyterian Church re – studied some of its strict attitudes plus provided more interest in national or international problems.[7] According to an article in the Western People May 9th 1936; (page 2) the Mayo Churches with Clergymen were at Mullafarry, Ballycastle; Michael Brannagan, Ballina ; Thomas Armstrong, Dromore West; Matthew Kerr, Hollymount; James Love, Killala; David Rogers also John Wilson, Newport; Geo. S. Keegan, Turlough; Andrew Brown, Westport; John James Black, while the Ballaghadeereen ministry was vacant at that time.[8] The diminutive in Church services was reflected in the number of Presbyterians in North Connacht during the early decades of the century acknowledged by the General Assembly; 'They are slowly diminishing in numbers and move away to more congenial surroundings. The Presbyterian Congregation of North Mayo were long established while those in the South or West of the County originated in the mid – 19th Century. By 1900 there were eighty – seven Presbyterians families but numbers in 1920 had fallen to just thirty – eight while just nine families lived in area ten years later.[9]

Ministers

Prior to 1840 in Mayo occasional services were held by the Presbyterian Minister of Turlough, Castlebar. A deputation from the Presbytery in Dublin, namely Rev. James Horner and John Birch visited Westport town. The result of the inquiry was that Rev. Dr. Henry Cooke was sent to officiate for a few 'Sabbaths' which were

4 www.ulsternationalist.freeservers.com/custom.html
5 https://www.familysearch.org/wiki/en/Ireland_Presbyterian_Church_Records
6 http://www.presbyterianhistoryireland.com/history/presbyterians-and-the-irish-language/
7 Mayo History & Society' (2015); Moran, Gerard & Ó Muraile, Nolláig.
8 History of Mayo' Vol 5, (2002); Quinn J. F.
9 Mayo History & Society' (2015) Moran, Gerard & Ó Muraile, Nolláig.

held in the Market House granted by George Clendening Esq. Following Cooke's transfer the congregation was favoured with the services of Rev. John Beckley, Monaghan, Rev. John Johnson, Tullylish also Rev. Henry Dobbin of Lurgan. During 1923 the congregation was formally organised by the Synod of Ulster. Robert Creighton was the first Minister ordained by the Presbytery of Dublin in Westport on December 23rd, 1823 with an Oath of Allegiance administered by the Marquis of Sligo and George Clendening Esq. The report to the Dublin Presbytery stated that the Marquis and Marchioness of Sligo with their family were attentive auditors at the Ordination! Rev. Creighton's demise occurred on October 31st, 1834. A three year gap ensued as the Congregation welcomed periodic visits from; Rev. William Graham of Dundonald D.D..also Dr. John Gill, Richard Gill plus L. K. Leslie. At a visitation held during 1838 by the Elders of Westport were James Pinkerton and Joseph McGreery, as Commissioners for the congregation were Joseph McGreery Jnr. with Patrick Louth. On June 14th, 1837 Mr. James Smith was ordained prior to a transfer to Galashiels, Scotland on September 20th, 1945. Rev. Smith was succeeded by David Adair who was ordained on May 8th, 1846 but died of smallpox on June 19th, 1854. The next Minister was the famous Richard Smyth, ordained on June 20th, 1855 who resigned on April 7th, 1857 to become minister of First Derry – a Doctor of Divinity (Glasgow 1871) – Professor of Oriental Literature and Hermeneutics (1865 – 70), Theology in Magee College, Derry and MP for Co. Derry 1874 – 78). Rev. Richard Smyth took an active stance with M. Sullivan Esq, MP in promoting the Irish Sunday Closing Act.[10] The fifth Minister to lead Westport's community was John James Black (later LL. D.) He stayed two years from his ordination on September 8th, 1857 to May 3rd, 1859 when he accepted a position to Ormond Quay Church, Dublin. His successor was the first ordained Minister; Rev. William Frederick White of Fethard and Canada. He was installed on August 2nd, 1859; while in service within the town he arranged for schoolhouses to be built at Leenane, Killary Harbour and Clogher, the manse was enlarged, and the church fenced around. His resignation occurred on June 15th, 1874 with a transfer to Lucan, Co. Dublin. A licentiate followed. Joseph McKinstry was ordained on Jan 6th, 1875 but he moved to Drumm in April 6th, 1881. The local Congregation's next choice was Samuel Glasgow Crawford who was ordained on October 5th, 1881 who later moved to minister at New South Wales on Jan 6th, 1886. He was succeeded by Rev, Samuel Andrews from Portadown but he resigned for an overseas mission on June 1888. David Wark was ordained on November 27th, 1888 he remained until August 12th, 1891 with a transfer to Waterford. Rev, John Alexander Bain of Raphoe was the tenth Minister who was installed with both Westport and Newport under his charge on June 22nd, 1892. He was presented with a D. D. by the Presbyterian Theological Faculty of Ireland during 1916. His resignation on April 1st, 1919 brought a new grouping together namely; Ballina, Westport, Newport, Castlebar and Hollymount. Rev. Ernest Hamiliton Williamson was installed in Westport on

10 'Castlebar – Co. Mayo - The Kirk & Other Presbyterian Churches in Mayo'.

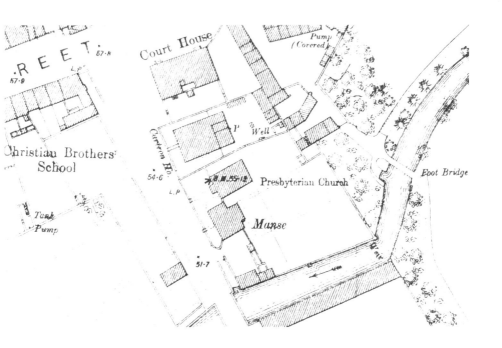

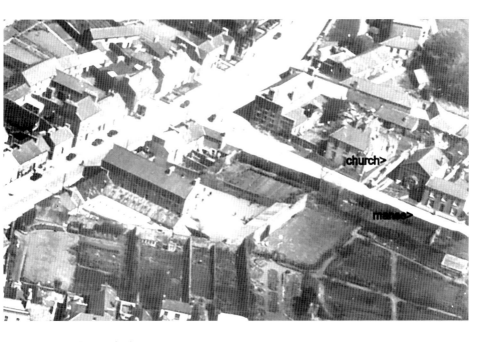

Pictures courtesy Seamus Gavin

March 8th, 1925. When he resigned on February 25th, 1942 the ministry was called Ballina and Dromore West.[11] Unfortunately, no details are available regarding ministers from the 1940s.

Congregation

In Westport Town during 1830 the Marquis of Sligo granted a site for the erection of a church and manse; these buildings were completed soon after.[12] The Presbyterian building was formally located on Kirk Street – now Distillery Road. By 1831 there were approx. thirty five members at their recently built Meeting House. During his 1840 visit to Westport William Thackeray wrote; 'There is a large Presbyterian church very well attended.' In the Cathair na Mart's 2017 edition of Ó Flanagáin's work; Appendix 2; the '1837 Topographical Dictionary of Ireland 'by Samual Lewis for the Aughaval Parish it portrays the following statistics regarding religious denominations; that 'a Presbyterian House had recently been built at Distillery Road (Kirk Lane) and a resident minister conducted service to thirty – forty parishioners twice on Sundays and once on Friday evenings.'[13] There is a mention of the Presbyterian Church of 1856; 'There are also places of worship for Presbyterians in connection with the Synod of Ulster, of the third class.'[14] The 1911 Irish Census listed 33% of Demesne employees were of the Presbyterian religion.[15] Joe Mc Nally wrote in his 'Westport; The Tear & The Smile' that the old church building was converted into Social Welfare offices during the 1950's with a new residence owned by the Corcoran family now on the Church site.[16]

I actually remember a Dispensary on the site with actual graves beside it. With the passage of time, regretfully, the church and congregation have been forgotten; it is the author's wish that this article will elicit a response with memories or stories of the Westport members of the Congregation or their Ministers. We owe them a debt of gratitude; it is important to acknowledge these people from an earlier era in the history of Westport town.

Gratitude is extended to Alicia Knox for information supplied from the Presbyterian Church of Ireland Assembly, Belfast and also Maureen Costello, Mayo County Library for assistance.

---

11 *The Presbyterian Church in Ireland; 'A Popular Study of the Presbyterians of Ireland'*
12 *The Presbyterian Church in Ireland; 'A Popular Study of the Presbyterians of Ireland'*
13 *Cathair na Mart, Journal of Westport Historical Society (1983); 'History of Westport' by Ó Flanagáin, Peadar BA. BComm;*
14 *Cathair na Mart, Journal of Westport Historical Society (2006 /2007); no 25.*
15 *Cathair na Mart, Journal of Westport Historical Society (2000); no 20.*
16 *'Westport; The Tear & The Smile' (1998); McNally Joe. Page 145.*

Footnotes

A Timeline of Presbyterianism in Ireland is available on;[17] www.presbyterianhistoryireland.com/history/timeline-for-presbyterianism-in-ireland/

'The initial appearance within the twenty – six counties of Ireland was in connection with the University of Dublin by Queen Elizabeth. The oldest congregation was on Wood Street and ministered by Dr. John Owen until 1947.' Remarks by Rev. Professor Barkley John M. MA PhD DD FR Hist. S. published by Publications Board, Presbyterian Church in Ireland, Church House, Belfast. The earliest period of Irish Presbyterian history 1603 – 30 has been described as 'Prescopalian' by Professor A. F. Scott Pearson. F. A. Angus, has written of Archbishop Laud's disciple Wentworth (later Earl of Stafford) 'That it is clear the Church of Ireland would either have withered away altogether or at best survived as an insignificant body in a few places if Stafford had not busied himself with its renewal.' [18]

A brief sketch by Revs. Dr. Latimer, David Stewart, J. B. Woodburn, A. Albert Campbell plus the Compiler J. W. K. may be read on this site.[19]

May be read free online; 'Ulster Presbyterianism; The Historical Perspective 1610 – 1970' by Peter Brooke; 'Truth will Prevail; The Rise of the Church of Jesus Christ of latter – day souls in the British Isles' by V. A. Bloxham, J. R. Moss, L. C. Porter. (Irish Economic & Social History Vol. 15 (1988) pages 133 – 135 [20]

Sources

A Study of the Methodist Community in Westport & surrounding area, County Mayo 1784 – 1961 with particular reference to the years 1847 – 1943. (1999); Evans Rosemary Pages 23 – 43.

A History of Congregations in the Presbyterian Church in Ireland 1610 – 1982. Belfast Ireland; Presbyterian Historical Society of Ireland, (1982).

Cathair na Mart, Journal of Westport Historical Society (1983); 'History of Westport' by Ó Flanagáin, Peadar BA. BComm; No.3; Pages 23 & 26 – 29.

Cathair na Mart, Journal of Westport Historical Society (2000); 'A History of Congregations in the Presbyterian Church in Ireland 1610 – 1982.' Evans, Rosemary. No. 20; Pages 27 & 39.

Cathair na Mart, Journal of Westport Historical Society (2006 / 7); Page 48.

Cathair na Mart Historical Journal (2017); 'Topographic Dictionary of Ireland' 1837 by Lewis, Samuel. No. 34; Page 51.

'History of Mayo' Vol 5, (2002); Quinn J. F.

'Mayo History & Society' (2015); Moran Gerard & Ó Muraile Nolláig.

The Presbyterian Church in Ireland; 'A Popular Study of the Presbyterians of Ireland' Holmes Finley, Darton, Longman & Todd Ltd, (2000), Page 168.

'Westport; The Tear & The Smile' (1998); McNally Joe. Page 145.

lisburn.com/books/history-presbyterian/history-presbyterian-1.html

https://www.britannica.com/topic/Presbyterian-Church in Ireland)

---

https://www.catholicireland.net/
https://www.familysearch.org/wiki/en/Ireland_Presbyterian_Church_Records
https://www.jstor.org/stable/24337364
https://www.libraryireland.com/ScotchIrishSeeds/VI-4.php
www.castlebar.ie/Nostalgia/The-Kirk-other-Presbyterian-churches-in-Mayo.shtml
www.presbyterianireland.org/
www.presbyterianhistoryireland.com/history/timeline-for-presbyterianism-in-ireland/
http://www.presbyterianhistoryireland.com/history/presbyterians-and-the-irish-language/
www.presbyterianhistoryireland.com/history/brief-biographies-irish-presbyteriens-1915/
www.ulsternationalist.freeservers.com/custom.html

Noelene Beckett Crowe as a poet / writer has had several articles published in numerous magazines, periodicals, journals plus ezines. An avid reader / writer, among her other interests are history, genealogy, research plus participating in many MOOC's online. She is a Committee member of Westport Historical Society plus Secretary of Mayo Genealogy Group. Her contributions to the latter's project; '101 Mayo People' may be found at www.ouririshheritage.org. The book: Kathleen Kilbane;: 'The Little Saint' of Achill Island, written by Allan Worthy / Victor Kennedy also features her literary work. She recites her poem at the Dedication of the Rockies on YouTube at Westport Covie Week 2016: www.youtube.com/watch?v=dtGOlnWdfIw
Email: noelenebc@gmail.com.

Ballycroy National Park. *Pic. Courtesy of Bill Murphy.*

THE MAYO ECHOSPHERE IN 2019[1]
(AFTER TIM ROBINSON)

Dr John O'Callaghan

There's music in the sighing of a reed;
There's music in the gushing of a rill;
There's music in all things, if men had ears;
Their earth is but an echo of the spheres.[2]

1 *Robinson, Tim, My Time in Space, Dublin, The Lilliput Press, 2001, pp. 173-206; Robinson, Tim, 'The Irish Echosphere in 2003', New Hibernia Review, 7:3 (Autumn 2003) pp. 9-22; Robinson, Tim, Connemara, The Last Pool of Darkness, Penguin Ireland (Dublin) 2008, p. 146.*
2 *Byron, George Gordon (Lord Byron), 1788-1824, the lines are from Don Juan, canto 15, stanza 5, written in 1823 and regarded as containing the 'earliest recorded use of the term "guide-book"', see Hooper, Glenn, Travel Writing and Ireland, 1760-1860, Culture, History, Politics, Palgrave Macmillan (Houndmills and New York) 2005, p. 108.*

The way nature is perceived in Ireland can vary dramatically from person to person.[3] In the current terminology the view is either biocentric or anthropocentric. To some, a wild, uncultivated tract of land may be eyed up with the thought of reclaiming it for farming, livestock rearing, building an airport or siting wind turbines; whereas to others it is an unspoiled wilderness that should be left alone rather than trying to alter it. In this essay I want to describe how one Yorkshireman, John Harvey Ashworth, writing about Ballycroy and environs in the early 1850s, came to influence another Yorkshireman, Tim Robinson, writing about Connemara and Árainn in the 1990s/2000s. The story that emerges shows how little attitudes to nature, land and culture in the west of Ireland have changed in the intervening century-and-a-half. What is even more extraordinary is that today there is a perfect opportunity to avoid repeating the mistakes of the past and help steer Ballycroy National Park and the area now known as Wild Nephin towards a sustainable future for the collective enjoyment of successive generations of Irish people.

The story begins in a book published anonymously in 1851 called The Saxon in Ireland, or, the rambles of an Englishman in search of a settlement in the west of Ireland.[4] It is now widely accepted that the author was Rev. John H. Ashworth. His middle name has been variously quoted as Henry, Harvey and Hervey but Harvey would appear to be the correct one as this is how he is named in the Oxford University graduates list and in a Directory of Modern English Biography compiled by Frederic Boase[5], published in 1892.

Tim Robinson refers to him as John Henry Ashworth and the Landed Estates Database[6] records him as John Hervey Ashworth, a possible typographical error and also the name pencilled into the title page of the online version of his book.[7]

---

3 Foster, John Wilson, (ed.) Nature in Ireland: A Scientific and Cultural History, Lilliput Press (Dublin) 1997.
4 Ashworth, John Harvey, The Saxon in Ireland, or, The Rambles of an Englishman in Search of a Settlement in the West of Ireland, London, John Murray, 1851. The title will be abbreviated to "The Saxon" for the remainder of the essay.
5 Boase, Frederic, Modern English Biography Containing Many Thousand Concise Memoirs Of Persons Who Have Died Since the Year 1850, With An Index Of The Most Interesting Matter; Volume 1, A-H; Truro, Netherton and Worth, 1892. Accessed from https://www.gutenberg.org/files/55059/55059-h/55059-h.htm on 15/01/2019. ASHWORTH, Rev. John Harvey (younger son of John Ashworth). b. Elland, Yorkshire 1795; ed. at Manchester gr. sch. and Univ. coll. Ox., scholar 1815, B.A. 1819, M.A. 1825; R. of Hethe, Oxon 1820–21; C. of St. Mary's, Rochdale 1821; bought old castle of Craggan, Co. Clare which he restored; V. of St. Mary's, Staveley-in-Cartmel 1874 to death; author of Hurstwood, a tale 3 vols. 1823; Scenes and thoughts from secluded life 2 vols. 1827; The Saxon in Ireland 1851; The young curate or the quicksand's of life [anon.] 1859, and Rathlynn [anon.] 3 vols. 1864. d. 4 Aug. 1882. [Author's note: C = curate; V = vicar]. Also, the list of electors for County Clare (1860-1) and the 1863 edition of Burke's Landed Gentry of Great Britain and Ireland lists him as John Harvey Ashworth. I acknowledge Marie Boran Of the Hardiman Library, NUIG, for these latter two findings.
6 See http://landedestates.nuigalway.ie/LandedEstates/jsp/family-show.jsp?id=507, accessed 15/01/2019.
7 See https://archive.org/details/saxoninireland00ashw/page/n7, accessed on 15/01/2019.

The particular passage in "The Saxon" where the figure of the Echo Hunter is introduced is in a story related to Ashworth by another, recently-arrived English settler, identified solely as 'Mr. S', whom the author, Ashworth, has befriended, and it is reproduced here:

> I was at Ballina, sitting at the open window of the inn, when the melodious sounds of a bugle, playing a beautiful Irish air, attracted my attention. No long time had elapsed when a little dapper-looking gentleman, of middle age, entered the room, with bugle in his hand. 'I have to thank you, sir, I presume,' said I, rising and bowing, 'for the great treat I have just enjoyed?' 'You have to thank me very little, sir,' replied he, carelessly; 'This instrument is all very well, but I seldom use it except to rouse Dame Nature, whom you will find sleeping among the crags and cliffs. The moment I sound my bugle, an answer comes from the mountains, no less singular than beautiful, leaping from rock to rock, now loud, now murmuring, but always sweet.'

> 'Excuse my dullness,' said I, smiling; 'I understand you now; you mean the echo.' 'Why yes,' he replied, 'echoes according to the common language of the world; I call them the voice of awakened nature. There is nothing in the theory of sound that can satisfactorily account to me for the wonderful voices my bugle has awakened in certain spots which I have discovered; but I do not make them generally known, for – laugh if you will – I have a notion, which I like to encourage, that Nature loves solitude, and would ill brook the being disturbed by every common idler. I have travelled through and through Ireland, meeting with such echoes in many a sequestered nook, unnoticed by any one before me, but Ballycroy, yes, sir, not twelve miles from hence – Ballycroy exceeds them all. But,' said he, lowering his voice, 'it were vain for you or any other mortal to attempt to find out these peculiar spots. I alone discovered them, and with me the knowledge of their existence will die.'

Ere we parted for the night, he invited me to accompany him on the following morning on an excursion into the Ballycroy mountains. He placed me on a certain spot; and exacting a promise that I would not follow him, he retired, and in about a quarter of an hour gave me such a treat in his peculiar art as I can never forget. The rocks and mountains seemed alive with harmony; the softest and wildest notes floated in the air, now close, now distant; now dying away in some distant recess of the valley, now awakening louder and louder among the cliffs and precipices; at one moment faint as the whisper of the breeze, at another loud and bold as the trumpet of the Archangel. I never before or since experienced the sensations which at that time overpowered me, and I no longer either smiled or wondered at the zeal of my new acquaintance in his peculiar and eccentric pursuit.' [8]

---

8 *My Time in Space, p.174/5.*

In addition, at this point, Ashworth provides the following information on precisely where the Echo Hunter evokes his best responses and consequently the location of Mr S's estate is (almost) revealed:

> 'it was in the wilder districts of Connaught and Munster that he most delighted. In Glen Inagh, not far from the head of Kylemore Lake, at the foot of Mulrea mountain, near the Killeries on the western side of Croagh Patrick, and in Ballycroy, near the lake of Carrig-a-binniogh, and in a spot between Corslieve and Nephinbeg mountains, he had awakened, he said, responses that might almost be thought superhuman: the valleys and cliffs seemed to start into life, and their voices were lifted up as if they were living things.' [9]

From accounts given elsewhere in the book of Ashworth's rambles with 'Mr. S', it is clear that the latter's farm, 'The Farm of Glen Duff', was most likely located, at least in part, in the townland of Maumaratta (Mám an Ráta, the col or mountain pass of the young hares). Maumaratta comprises much of the catchment area of the Owenduff river, a Special Area of Conservation, intersected by the Bangor Trail and situated to the west of the Nephinbeg mountain range. Fr. Seán Noone states that an 'old hunting lodge at Gleann Dubh [in Maumaratta]' was occupied by a Keane family of herders into the early 1900s.[10]

At a later stage in 'The Saxon', after an extended (easterly) bog trot across 'Maumarattah', the author and Mr. S would appear to arrive at a point where the Mountain Meitheal shelter now stands on the Bangor Trail: 'and skirting the uninteresting shores of Lough Avoher, which lies embosomed in a vale under the craggy heights of Letterkeen, we passed the smaller Lough Gaul' - this may possibly be Lough Gall or Geal on current maps[11] - 'and thus, having well examined the beauties and capabilities of this terra incognita, we seriously set our faces towards the farm of Glenduff.'[12] He goes on to state that it was late in the evening when they arrived back there, which would appear to indicate they had still an hour or two more north of Loughs Avoher and Gaul/Gall/Geal to go before reaching the farm, possibly pinpointing it closer to the Bangor Erris/Bellacorrick area.

As Ashworth is at pains to remain anonymous himself and in turn keep the identity of Mr. S and 'The farm of Glenduff' hidden from his readers, it is difficult to discern with certainty where the 'S' family lived. Perhaps a more thorough search of the census data for the 1835 to 1865 period may reveal their identities as we also learn

---

9 op. cit. The Saxon in Ireland, p.205.

10 Noone, Seán Fr., Where the Sun Sets: Ballycroy, Belmullet, Kilcommon & Kiltane County Mayo, The Leinster Leader, Naas, 1991, p. 51.

11 See, for example, Wild Nephin, 1:25,000 scale map featuring Wild Nephin Wilderness Area, Ballycroy National Park, Great Western Greenway, East/West Mapping, (Enniscorthy) 2015 where the lake is named 'Geal' and OSI Discovery Series # 23, 4th edition, scale 1:50,000, 2010, where it is named Lough Gall.

12 op. cit. The Saxon in Ireland, p. 233.

from Ashworth that the 'S's' had 6 children, including two sons, Frank and Edwin and a daughter, Catherine. The eldest, unnamed son was living in England in 1850. An additional 'clue', that may be an error on Ashworth's part, as this author can find no trace of it on any map or reference to it in any literature, is that the farm was close to a holy well dedicated to St. Kiaran (sic).

Returning to his encounters with the Echo Hunter, Mr. S was so moved by the bugler's performance that he purchased land in Ballycroy and following 'improvements', i.e. what we now call land reclamation, he converted the wilderness into valuable farmland. [Note: He was already living in this area for 14-15 years when Ashworth met him.] This is a significant piece of information as it gives an indication of the extent of the human impact upon the heart of the Wild Nephin area in the past. Mr. S met the Echo Hunter only one more time[13] after their first encounter:

'When I last caught sight of him, he was leaning pensively against the rock, round whose base we turn on entering the glen below us. Our greeting was short. He congratulated me upon my improvements but declared significantly that "Art would drive out Nature". 'This', he said, 'is my last visit to this valley; it was once a favourite spot of mine, but the presence of man has tainted it. In Corranabinna I am safe from intrusion. There man will never pitch his tent; it is too near the sky; and let me tell you sir, Nature speaks there in a language that even these rocks could never equal.' I could not prevail upon him to accept the rude hospitalities of my cottage and after we had parted about ten minutes, a few discordant notes of his bugle awakened a thousand more discordant echoes, and I never saw him more!'

The story of the Echo Hunter may be purely allegorical, nonetheless its theme still holds true today. To some a wilderness or a 'waste land' is there to be cultivated and 'improved', while to others it is Nature at its finest and deserves to be left alone for Nature's sake as well as for the continuing enjoyment of other living organisms.

In what was to become a recurring theme in Tim Robinson's writings, an essay entitled 'The Echosphere' first appeared in 2001 in his collection My Time in Space[14]. Robinson's subsequent version of his essay, entitled 'The Irish Echosphere in 2003' appeared in New Hibernia Review.[15] Both versions contain a homage to Roundstone Bog, a terrain that holds a special place in Robinson's heart. He 'became aware of [Roundstone Bog] through the writings of the naturalist Robert Lloyd Praeger even before [he] came to live in Roundstone itself'[16] and 'it was one of the factors' behind his settling there in 1984. Both essays contain most of the above extended

13 If any readers know of such a well, I should be delighted to hear about it.
14 Robinson, Tim, My Time in Space, Dublin, The Lilliput Press, 2001, pp. 173-206.
15 Robinson, Tim, The Irish Echosphere in 2003, New Hibernia Review, vol. 7, no. 3, Autumn 2003, pp. 9-22.
16 op.cit. My Time in Space, p.179.

quotations from The Saxon in Ireland, 'trimmed'[17] in parts to exclude irrelevant details. Robinson credits Ashworth's tale of the Echo Hunter as his source and inspiration for the neologism 'echosphere' that he coined to epitomise 'zone[s] in which a balance is maintained between culture and the wild'.[18]

In 2019, almost 170 years after The Saxon in Ireland was written, this wild and remote part of west Mayo is in the spotlight again, for all the right reasons. Ballycroy National Park became Ireland's 'newest' national park in 1998. It is currently under study with a view to rewilding part of it it as Ireland's last remaining wilderness.[19] In July 2018, the Irish Government launched 'a major new plan, so that Irish and international visitors can look forward to an enhanced experience at Ireland's National Parks and Reserves.' 'Experiencing the Wild Heart of Ireland, A Tourism Interpretative Masterplan for Ireland's National Parks and Coole Garryland Nature Reserve', was published jointly by Josepha Madigan TD, Minister for Culture, Heritage and the Gaeltacht, and Brendan Griffin TD, Minister of State for Tourism and Sport. The press release at the launch stated: 'The interpretative masterplan is a product of the Department of Culture, Heritage and the Gaeltacht and Fáilte Ireland's strategic partnership. It sets out a framework that will guide the phased development of enhanced visitor centre experiences and improved visitor facilities at Ireland's National Parks and Reserves, based on research into international best practice. The work will be funded jointly by the Department of Culture, Heritage and the Gaeltacht and Fáilte Ireland through a multi-million Euro investment package over the coming years.'

The features of the plan include:
· Capturing the special and unique stories of each National Park and Nature Reserve and bringing them to life for visitors
· Leverage the collective value of the National Parks, particularly those along the Wild Atlantic Way, where five of the six parks are located, and increasing their appeal to visitors.
· Using international best practice to improve the visitor experience in the National Parks' Visitor Centres.

It is difficult to predict what National Parks and Wildlife Service (NPWS) will 'do' with Ballycroy National Park. The specific recommendations in the plan include the erection of a Dark Skies Planetarium and Night Sky Observatory and enhancing the Visitor Centre and services provided to include more 'interpretative space'. If or when the park is promoted by Fáilte Ireland as 'Ireland's last wilderness', ever-

---

17 Robinson's term.
18 op.cit. Robinson, Tim, Connemara, The Last Pool of Darkness, Penguin Ireland (Dublin) 2008, p. 146.
19 See, for example, O'Callaghan, John, Rewilding Ireland? The Wild Nephin Wilderness Project, Co. Mayo, M.A. Thesis, NUIG, 2017 and Consultants' reports on Wild Nephin, commissioned by NPWS (in preparation).

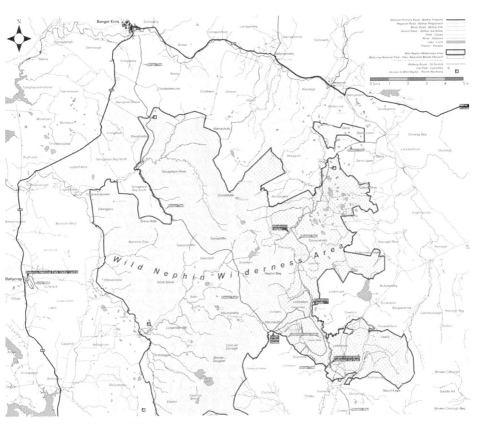

Figure I: *Map of Wild Nephin Wilderness Area*

increasing numbers of tourists will want to visit and experience it and suddenly it may not be a wilderness anymore. This is a paradox that cannot be avoided and is a recurring theme in much of the 'New Nature Writing' emanating from both Britain and Ireland in recent years.

In the opinion of one of Ireland's foremost nature writers, Michael Viney, 'Wild Nephin won't work if it is managed like any other [national] park.'[20]   However, if NPWS were to 'manage' it safely through a period of transition and then simply let it be and allow time for nature to do its own rewilding, this, I contend, would be the best option.[21]   Once the area of Ballycroy National Park now known as Wild Nephin is left to its own devices and 'Mother Nature' permitted to take her own course, then in twenty, or fifty years' time, it will truly be regarded as a wilderness where the 'Echo-hunters' of the future can roam free.

---

20 *Viney, Michael, Irish Times, 6 Jan 2018.*
21 *https://www.theguardian.com/environment/2019/jan/17/country-diary-what-happens-when-nature-takes-back-control-woodland-birds-durham-city, accessed 08/02/2019.*

Biographical Note: Tim Robinson was born in Yorkshire in 1935. He studied maths at Cambridge and then worked for many years as a visual artist in Istanbul, Vienna and London. In 1972 he moved to Inis Mór, in the Aran Islands. Stones of Aran: Pilgrimage, published in 1985, won the Irish Book Award Literature Medal and a Rooney Prize Special Award for Literature in 1987. Stones of Aran: Labyrinth appeared in 1995 and Setting Foot on the Shores of Connemara was published in 1996. My Time in Space followed in 2001, containing a number of autobiographical essays and personal philosophies and a collection of stories and speculative essays, Tales and Imaginings, appeared the following year in 2002. He is also the author of the widely-acclaimed trilogy: Connemara: Listening to the Wind (2006); Connemara: The Last Pool of Darkness (2008) and Connemara: A Little Gaelic Kingdom (2011).

Dr. John O'Callaghan received an M.A. in Irish Studies from NUIG in 2017. His thesis was entitled Rewilding Ireland? The Wild Nephin Wilderness Project, Co. Mayo. It was he who successfully nominated Westport in The Irish Times as The Best Place to Live in Ireland. He lives in Ennis, Co. Clare.

TWO EARLY CHRISTIAN MONUMENTS AT AUGHAGOWER, CO. MAYO

Jim Higgins M.A., Ph.D.

Introduction

Two Early Christian monuments at Aughagower are published for the first time and are discussed in some detail. Another monument of 12th century date from this site, (an early medieval cross) has previously been published by the writer (Higgins 2004-5, 53-58). The two monuments described below represent an earlier strata of archaeological heritage at the site. A tau or T-shaped cross at the site may have been either a boundary or termon marker or a funerary monument. It is set in a partial base of stone, only some of which seems to survive. The second early monument is now incomplete pillar stone with a pair of bosses projecting from its sides and a crudely cut, encircled cross on one of its broad faces. This monument too, may have had any of the above-mentioned functions. This latter monument can be paralleled among Irish and Scottish monuments (Higgins 1987, 58-9) and in particular among a series of bossed pillar stones found around the perimeters of the monastic site at Manistir Ciarán, Inishmór, Árainn (Aran Islands), and is an unpublished monument from Templedearg in Connemara (Higgins, forthcoming), and on Árdoileán (High Island), Co. Galway.

The Tau Cross (Plate 1)

Plate 1 – Tau Cross with partial hollowed base. Photograph: J. Higgins.

In an isolated section of the graveyard across the road from the main site, there is, a rough sandstone T-shaped or Tau Cross. It is unclear whether this is in its original position but given the presence of a multi-piece base into which the cross has been set it may be in situ. Most of the basal stone is covered and it is possible that two of these elements of a cross-base once occurred and that they wrapped around the base of the stone in the manner of a two-piece socket. The cross may originally have been used either as a termon marker or as a funerary monument.

The stone seems to have been deliberately fashioned to a T-shape and there are no stumps or other indications which might suggest it to have been an ordinary Latin Cross the head of which has become broken away.

The cross measures about 70cms in width across its arms and some 56cms or so of this length presently shows above the general ground level of the cemetery. The object is simply and crudely made and has no form of decoration which might provide dating evidence for this stone. Most Tau-shaped crosses are of Early Christian or Early Historic date, (that is, from the period between, say, the 6th and 12th centuries). In recent years, such crosses have been found in increasing numbers as a result of fieldwork, though they are still relatively uncommon. Their distribution is mainly concentrated in the west of Ireland.

Some features of this example may indicate that this one is of Early Christian date. The thick growth of lichen and moss is an indication of some antiquity but is no proof of age. The notched stone which forms a collar-like socket around its base is however reminiscent of the same cross-bases which occur on Early Historic and Early Medieval crosses. Examples occur at Glendalough, Co. Wicklow. It is difficult to be sure whether the single identifiable stone which formed the partial socket at the bottom of the stone was (A) originally a larger socketed stone with a rectangular hold in the middle of (B) one of a pair of stones which when placed together fitted snugly around the base of the shaft of the Tau cross. Two notched stones originally formed this basal socket. Unfortunately, the surviving 'half notched' stone is the only one visible and it is mostly covered over. Only excavation could indicate whether the socket stone was a single stone or two stones or whether the base is decorated or inscribed. Simply perforated bases sometimes of thin slabs so various shapes - rectangular, square, sub-rectangular, oblong (or irregular) occur on several Early Christian sites at Inishkea North, High Island (Árd Oileán) they are also common on Iona in Scotland. There are several bases one of type (A) (two notched slabs) and the other of type (B) a single slab with a rectangular perforation. The stones are now lying loose on the sand hills near the various cross slabs and huts on the island, some of which were excavated by Françoise Henry.

At Iniscealtra, Co. Clare, some of the cross-slabs and pillar-stones are still in situ in socketed stones at the head and foot of graves. In some cases, inscribed and cross decorated recumbent stones have further cross decorated slabs or pillar-stones set in socket holes in them. At the cemetery at Reefert Church, Glendalough, Co. Wicklow socketed Early Christian bases and recumbent slabs have plain crosses, cross decorated pillar-stones and cross slabs set in them.

The parallels cited above (and others) all suggest that the Tau-shaped stone at Aghagower may well be of Early Christian or Early Historic date and may in fact be in situ (as some of the parallels cited above are). Whether this tau-shaped cross was erected as a gravestone, a boundary marker or for some other function is unknown. It might also have been a termon marker, a dedicatory monument or a funerary marker.

The Tau-shaped stone at Aughagower is not the only Co. Mayo example to be found recently. In the last few years several have been recognised within the county. Mayo is rapidly emerging as a county where a very large number of Early Christian or Early Historic funerary monuments continue to be found as fieldwork by amateur and professional archaeologists and historians continues to reveal more of the county's past.

Plain, Tau-shaped crosses have also been found in cemeteries at Shrule and Kilmovee, Co. Mayo and these are among a group of Early Christian carvings which include cross inscribed stones as well as plain tau-shaped crosses. Several of these carvings are the topic of a forthcoming article (Higgins forthcoming). There are plain examples of Tau-shaped crosses from Tory Island, Co. Donegal which was possibly a termon marker[1] of some sort and is located among a variety of other fragments on a leacht near the round tower in West Town[2]. The Tory Island tau cross is of large size measuring 1m 90cms high and 40cms across. It is the largest of the Irish free-standing crosses. Like the Aughagower example the stone is crudely shaped with no elaboration. Two more tau-shaped crosses occur at Kilmalkedar, County Kerry.

Another good plain example occurs at Carrownaseer North, Co. Galway. The only ornate example in stone from Ireland is the well-known tau-shaped cross from Killinaboy, Co. Clare with its carved human heads at each end of the top of the arm. That example is Romanesque in style, and it is probably of 12th century date or may date to circa 1200A.D. (Rynne (1967), 146-165).

A broken Latin cross at Drumhallagh Lower near Rathmullan, Co. Donegal has carvings of a tau-shaped and a spiral ended crozier on the same side of the stone.

---

1 *Higgins 1987, pp. 24-5 and Fig. 7c.*
2 *Lacy, B. et al. (1983), Site No. 1620 (No. 1), pp. 296-8 and Plate 61, 297.*

Tau-shaped croziers are also represented on several of Ireland's high crosses. The Doorty Cross at Kilfenora has ecclesiastics holding three types of crozier. The Irish drop-looped, continental spiral-ended and Tau-shaped croziers are all represented on the same high cross. The Market Cross at Kells, Co. Meath also has a representation of a tau-shaped crozier.

Tau-shaped crosses of Early Christian or Early Historic period (approximately 6th to 12th century) are still relatively rare but an increasing number of them are now being discovered. Unfortunately, they are notoriously difficult to date unless they have some carved feature or other distinctive attribute. There was an apparent revival of the use of Tau Crosses in some places in the 18th or 19th century. Some Co. Galway and Co. Mayo cemeteries have numbers of plain examples which, to judge by the numbers which occur, their relative lack of weathering and their ordering as part of the 'top layer' of funerary monuments within their cemeteries.

A further plain, roughly trimmed stone of Tau-shape occurs at Carownaseer North Townland near Dunmore, Co. Galway. This has been published elsewhere by the writer. The stone is very crudely worked, is 67cms high and 49cms in maximum width.[3]

At Kilmalkedar, Co. Kerry there are several plain tau-shaped stones some of them hitherto unrecorded. One of these is previously mentioned briefly in print.[4] One of the Kilmalkedar tau crosses is also published and illustrated in Cuppage et al. (1986).[5]

Some early Irish sundials including one at Kilmalkedar also have a vaguely tau-shaped form but this may be more for structural and functional reasons rather than from any attempt to deliberately adopt a tau-shaped form for such items.[6] A tau-shaped stone with a distinct dip in the centre of the middle of its upper limb was found by M.J. O'Kelly in his excavations at Church Island near Valencia, Co. Kerry.[7] O'Kelly judged this stone to be a gable finial and the central dip would seem to suggest that it was based on a "butterfly-shaped" gable-finial. A second stone found at the site is an actual butterfly gable finial. The writer has suggested elsewhere that the stone would seem too long, slender and thin to have served as a gable finial. Despite the dip in the centre of this upper limb which looks like an echo of the "wings" of a gable finial the object is still essentially a tau-shaped cross.[8]

---

3 *Higgins (1987) Vol. II Cat. No. 116 p.396 and Fig. 112 Plate 40c and discussion Vol. I., p.25*
4 *Higgins (1987), 25 passim.*
5 *See Cuppage, J. et al. (1986) for one of the Kilmalkedar, Co. Kerry tau-shaped stones (Site No. 855, Fig. 192(b)).*
6 *See ibid. (1986) Site 855, (No. 2 in text), 310-11 and Plate 29 and Fig. 183 for the Kilmalkedar sundial.*
7 *O'Kelly (1958), 97, Fig. 8 and pp. 94-6.*
8 *Higgins (1987), 25 and Fig. 7B, p.22.*

The most elaborate of the Irish tau-shaped crosses in stone is undoubtedly the Kilnaboy Cross from Co. Clare. This has been published in some detail by Rynne (1967).[9] This is an unusual and late example and is Romanesque in style and 12th century in date. The cross recalls, to a large degree, Romanesque heads such as those represented on the voussoirs of the Romanesque doorway at Dysart.O'Dea, for example, and in a detailed discussion, it has been shown convincingly that the stone is a relatively late example of a tau-shaped cross and certainly Ireland's most elaborate example of a free-standing features of this kind.[10]

Plain incised single line "Tau-crosses" are illustrated by Wakeman (1891). He illustrates what are simply tau-shaped configurations of a single-line rather than stones of a tau-shaped outline. One of Wakeman's examples was incised on a stone at Ballinacarrig, Co. Kerry.[11] Another occurred on a stone at Monksgrange, near Drogheda, Co. Louth.[12]

Some stones have representations of tau crosses carved on them. A free standing ringless cross of Early Christian type from Broughanlea, near Bonamargy, Co. Antrim has carved on its north face representations of two croziers one of which is crook headed while the second crozier is tau-shaped. These may, as Harbison suggests, "... possibly represent the croziers of Saints Paul and Anthony respectively."[13]

The crook-shaped cross on the Broughanlea stone may also represent the native form and the Eastern form of crozier. This would seem to be reflected in the representation of three different types of croziers which are depicted in the hands of three ecclesiastics carved on the Doorty Cross at Kilfenora, Co. Clare.[14]

Some later representations of tau-shaped crosses as distinct from tau-shaped stones occur but these are rare. A medieval representation of an actual tau-shaped crozier and a bell the former with metal fittings, knops and a pointed tip is carved in an incised manner on a grave slab in the graveyard and at Kilnaboy, Co. Clare.[15]

Only one tau-shaped crozier of these survives from Ireland in the form of the head of a crozier now in the National Museum of Ireland which is not provenanced.

Tau-shaped crosses are not very common in Ireland. Several seem from their context to date to the Early Christian or Early Historic period, that is sometime be-

---

9 For the Kilnaboy Cross see Rynne in Rynne (Ed.) (1967), pp. 146-165 and references therein.
10 Ibid., op. cit.
11 For the Ballinacarrig, Co. Kerry incised tau-shaped design see Wakeman (1891), Plate I, Fig. 11
12 For the Monksgrange near Drogheda, Co. Louth example see Wakeman (1891), Plate I, Fig. 10.
13 See Harbison (1992) Cat. No. 26 Figure 81, p.30 and references therein for the Roughanlea cross
14 Rynne (1967), ibid.
15 See Rynne (1967), ibid

tween the 5th and 12th centuries. Few examples with any elaborate carving occur, plain examples of probable Early Christian date have been discussed by the writer elsewhere (Higgins (1987)). Tau-shaped crosses in general have been discussed by Rynne (1967) who deals with the Romanesque one from Kilnaboy, Co. Clare in some detail. A head of an actual tau-shaped crozier of metal with dolphin-like finials from Co. Kilkenny is now in the National Museum. Another tau-shaped crozier is shown on a medieval slab from Kilnaboy, Co. Clare, (Rynne 1967).

Representations of ecclesiastics holding tau-shaped croziers occur on various high crosses and in some cases the "Eastern" tau-shaped crozier is shown held by one ecclesiastic and an Irish or Continental crook and spiral ended examples are held by other ecclesiastics (Rynne, 1967; Harbison 1992).

Altogether the tau-shaped stones or crosses, tau-croziers of metal and representations of tau-croziers on high crosses and later slabs from a very interesting group and span a wide date range. The occurrence of one at Aghagower is further evidence if it be needed for the importance of the site in the Early Historic period when the use of "unusual" cross forms may be taken as evidence of knowledge of forms widely used elsewhere in Europe.

The Bossed Pillarstone with Encircled Greek Cross (Plate 2 and 3)

Plate 2 - Fragmentary Bossed Cross. Photograph: J. Higgins.

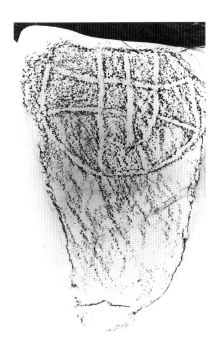

Plate 3 - Rubbing of Bossed Cross with Excised Cross. Photograph: J. Higgins.

This stone is incomplete, and its top is missing. The stone is a long, sub-rectangular slab with a pair of bosses projecting from the sides of the shaft. The main faces of the slab have been dressed flat and the sides of the stone have been curved and carefully dressed (and rounded off somewhat). The bottom of the stone is broken and one of the flat faces is carved with a crude encircled cross. This is irregular and looks incomplete. The arms of the cross are curved upwards and downwards above and below the top and bottom of the base respectively. The shaft of the cross is relatively straight and a third upright which curves inwards towards its lower end also occurs. It looks as if an inner curve was intended but never completed.

The stone measures 76cms in total height and varies between 58cms (including the two bosses). The shaft of the cross width just below the bosses. The bosses are 18.5cms and 21cms in height and average 7cms in width. The bossed feature can be paralleled widely, mainly on sites along the Irish coast in particular. Bosses on Early Christian crosses have been discussed in detail by the writer elsewhere (Higgins 1987). Small "ear-like" bosses projecting from the upper sides of crosses and common on Irish and some Scottish pillar stones and free standing crosses.[16] Small circular bosses projecting from the flat tops of slabs and crosses also occur

---

16 *Higgins (1987), pp. 58-59 and see Figs. 28, 29, 36A and 37 for crosses with bosses on their tops, sides and outer corners from Ireland and Scotland.*

in both areas. Semi-circular bosses projecting in the position of 'arms' are rarer but occur in some of the Termon Pillars on tall pillarstones found at Mainistir Ciarán, Árainn, (or Inish Mór) Oileán Árainn.17 Small bosses like primitive 'arms' also occur on a shaped stone at Templedearg near Clifden, Co. Galway. The latter stone is an Early Christian monument with a rounded head and grooved and bossed sides. It was reused and had an inscription carved on it in the 19th century (Higgins, forthcoming).

References

Corlett, C. (1999) Antiquities of Old Rathdown, Bray, 1999.

Corlett, C. (2003) "The Rathdown Slabs - Vikings and Christianity", Archaeology Ireland, Vol. 17, No. 4, Winter, 2003.

Cuppage, J. et al. (1986) Archaeological Survey of the Dingle Peninsula, Suirbhé Seandálaíochta Chorca Dhuibhna, Bally Ferriter, 1986.

Harbison, P. (1992) The High Crosses of Ireland: An Iconographical and Photographic Survey, 3 Volumes, Bonn, 1992.

Higgins, J. and McHugh, A. (1992) The White Friars Abbeytown, Cill-na-Manach, Galway, 1992.

Higgins, J. and Parsons, A. (1997) St. Mary's Cathedral Tuam, Its Restoration, History and Archaeology, Galway, 1996.

Higgins, J. (1987) The Early Christian Cross-Slabs, Pillar-Stones and Related Monuments of Co. Galway, Ireland, B.A.R., International Series, No. 375 I and II, Oxford, 2 Vols. 1987.

Higgins, J. (2004-5) "An Early Medieval Cross at Aughagower, Co. Mayo", Cathair na Mart, 24 (2004-5), 53-58.

Higgins, J. (forthcoming) "New Early Christian Monuments from Galway City and County", Galway Heritage / Oidhreacht na Gaillimhe, 2020.

Keville, J. (1983) "Aughagower" (continued) Cathair na Mart, Journal of the Westport Historical Society, Vol. 3, No. 1 (1983), pp. 3-24.

Mannion, B. (1988) "Aughagower and its Patrician sites and connections" Cathair na Mart, Journal of the Westport Historical Society, Vol. 8, No. 1, (1988), pp. 5-18.

Ó h-Éailidhe, P. (1957) "The Rathdown Slabs", J. Roy. Soc. Antiqs. Ireland, 87 (1957), pp. 75-88.

Ó h-Éailidhe, P. (1958) "Fassaroe and Associated Crosses", J. Roy. Soc. Antiqs. Ireland, 88 (1958), pp.101-10.

Ó h-Éailidhe, P. (1973) "Early Christian Grave Slabs in the Dublin Region", J. Roy. Soc. Antiqs. Ireland, 103 (1973), pp. 51-64.

Ó h-Éailidhe, P. (1984) "Decorated Stones at Kilgobbin, County Dublin", J. Roy. Soc.

---

17 *See Higgins, J. forthcoming 2011 for the Temple Dearg and other newly discovered monuments from Galway City and County in Galway's Heritage / Oidhreacht na Gaillimhe, Autumn/Winter 2019.*

Antiqs. Ireland, 114 (1984), pp. 142-4.

Ó h-Éailidhe,, P. and Prendergast (1977) "Two Unrecorded Graveslabs in County Dublin", J. Roy. Soc. Antiqs. Ireland, 107 (1977), pp. 139-42.

Rynne, E. (1967) "The Tau-Cross at Killinaboy; Pagan or Christian", in Rynne, E. (ed.) (1967) North Munster Studies. Essays in Commemoration of Monsignor Michael Moloney, Limerick 1967, pp. 146-165.

Wakeman, (1891) "On the Early Form of Incised Crosses", J. Roy. Soc. Antiqs. Ireland, (1891).

Wilde, W. (1867) Lough Coirib Its Shores and Islands, Dublin 1867 [This book has been republished in abridged form and more recently in facsimile under the title Wilde's Lough Corrib (note the change in spelling) by Kevin Duffy, Headford, 2003].

Dr Jim Higgins is Heritage Officer with Galway City Council.

CENTENARY STORIES
(1918 -2018)

Mary J. Murphy

Eva O'Flaherty's newly confirmed role in the founding of Cumann na mBan, and her links with Dr Arthur MacBride and with the influential senior Fenian from Tuam, Dr Mark Ryan. Also, the story of painter Marie Howet's fifty year love affair with Achill Island to be celebrated in a new book due for publication in 2020.

One hundred years ago two major nationalist figures who were both born within a stone's throw of Tuam – 'Achill's Eva O'Flaherty' and Dr. Mark Ryan – were at the heart of a combined Irish resistance to the Military Services Bill (Conscription), passed by the British Parliament on 18 April 1918. Dr. Ryan, whose life was commemorated in his birthplace of Kilconly near Tuam in September 2018,[1] was then still living in London, where he was in partnership with Dr. Arthur MacBride. He did not move back to Dublin to live with his sister Margaret in Glasnevin until 1924, but O'Flaherty had been making more regular peregrinations back and forth to her homeland from about 1907 onwards. Many of those trips had been to Achill Island, and of an artistic nature, some years before her co-founding there of the Scoil Acla summer school in 1910 with Mrs Emily Weddall et al. By 1918 Eva was at the silent heart of Cumann na mBan, and it was just confirmed in September 2018 that she was indeed on the founding committee of that organisation too – with Jennie Wyse Power, Agnes O'Farrelly, 'Cesca', Louise Gavan Duffy, Elizabeth Bloxham and Mary Maguire Colum - in 1914.

Eva was a close acquaintance of Dr. Ryan (1844-1940), an extremely influential senior IRB/Fenian, whose importance to 'the movement' (as a conduit for funds pouring eastwards back across the Atlantic from John Devoy & Co) was noted by WB Yeats as early as the late 1890s. Ryan was specifically mentioned as 'a close personal friend' of hers in her Irish Times obituary of April 1963 and had been inducted into the Fenians in his youth by Michael Davitt. Ryan shared a practice with Dr. Arthur MacBride, brother of Major John MacBride, and by 1937, in the wake of the Kirkintilloch tragedy, Ryan was once again in 'partnership' with Arthur MacBride, this time when both men served on an island committee – along with Eva O Flaherty, Catherine Glynn and many others – which was established to initiate industries on the island to keep workers at home.

---

1 At an event organised by Bride Brady and her industrious committee.

Portrait of Eva O'Flaherty in her Dooagh home by Derek Hill (1947).

Eva herself was born into nationalist 'royalty' in Lisdonagh House, Caherlistrane in 1874. Her mother, Mary Frances Barbara O'Gorman Lalor O'Flaherty, of the Ennis-Bunratty clan (who share common ancestry with Boris Johnson), was a descendant of prominent O'Gorman United Irishmen and Young Irelanders. Eva's father, Martin, had been sent to the US by Charles Gavan Duffy in 1848 as an 'agent' to raise money, arms and funds for the Young Ireland movement. O'Flaherty was a lawyer and well as a JP and a substantial landowner and had been part of John Mitchel's defence team for his Treason-Felony trial along with Robert Emmet's elderly barrister, Robert Holmes.

After her schooling at Mount Anville and Alexandra colleges in Dublin, Eva O'Flaherty trained in millinery and modelling in Paris, and by 1900 she was in the Gaelic League in London, where she lived on Chester Terrace, and had a millinery emporium on Sloane Street. She was also heavily involved in the United Irishwomen there along with fellow compatriots Mary Spring Rice and Anita Mac-Mahon et al. In the UK capital Eva rubbed shoulders with the likes of Pádraic Ó Conaire, Francesca 'Cesca' Chevenix Trench (Sadhbh Trinseach), Art Ó Briain, Major Dermot Freyer (subsequently of Corrymore House, whom she would live beside on Achill Island years later and one of whose sons was named Patrick Pearse Freyer) and mingled in the same GL circles as Eileen Costello of Tuam (the former Edith Stroud). Also, in the merry mix were Min Ryan (who was 'engaged' to Eva's pal, Sean MacDiarmada), Garret FitzGerald's mother, the formidable Mabel

McConnell, plus Darrell Figgis (another resident of Achill in 1913), and Colm Ó Lochlainn, who along with O'Flaherty, Figgis, MacMahon, Emily Weddall, Claude Chavasse was a co-founder of Scoil Acla.

London was where the seeds of nationalism and revolution were nourished in the run up to 1916, and Tuam was where Eva's great friend, Seán MacDiarmada was arrested by the local RIC chief, Comerford, under the Defence of the Realm Act in 1915. Just three years later she would find herself cycling around the streets of Dublin during the Easter Rising, on a 'courier' mission of some indeterminate sort, as MacDiarmada's clock wound down inside the GPO, until his eventual execution on 12 May 1916. Paul Henry, whom Eva seems to have known in the vibrant artistic milieu of Paris in the late 1890s, and who painted a portrait of her brother Arthur in 1916, was also in Dublin during the Rising. There is so much we still do not know about the extraordinary life of Eva O'Flaherty.[2] Anne Tierney of the OTS discovered a newspaper cutting which alluded to the fact that O'Flaherty was on the founding Committee of Cumann na mBan with Cesca and Jenny Wyse-Power, and then this writer discovered, in September 2018, Eva's name listed in the original Constitution of Cumann na mBan. So, there she was, our 'forgotten island heroine' at the heart of things at the very highest levels, as we had always suspected. We had known from Louise Gavan-Duffy's Witness Statement to the Bureau of Military History (No. 216) that Eva had been in the Cumann in Dublin in 1914 but discovering her name as a co-founder of the Cumann, catapulted her onto another level of involvement entirely.[3] That involvement came into sharp focus with Tierney's discovery of that newspaper cutting from a 1937 edition of the Kerry newspaper The Liberator which copper-fastened Eva's pivotal involvement with her fellow nationalist protagonists at the most senior levels in the run up to the Easter Rising on the twenty-first anniversary of that event.

So too did Dr. Hilary Pyle's allusions to Eva at a Centenary Lecture in O'Flaherty's home in the former St Colman's Knitting Industries on Achill in July 2016, where she referred to O'Flaherty as "the elusive lady", and in her (Pyle's) book, Cesca's Diary (2005), which also shone a light on Eva's vital importance in Cumann na mBan. On a number of occasions Cesca mentioned that members of the Cumann would have to get advice or information from 'Miss O'Flaherty', particularly with regard to divisive issues such as their stance on matters like Conscription, and the potential of a split in the Cumann with reference to Neutrality. (During that 1916 Centenary series of lectures Maria Gillen spoke on the life of Mrs Weddall, Dr Edward King made a presentation on the life of Darrell Figgis, and Sile McHugh spoke on the remarkable life of journalist Anita MacMahon).

---

2 *I merely scraped the surface of it in Achill's Eva O'Flaherty: Forgotten Island Heroine (2012), and new information has been constantly coming to light in the intervening years.*
3 *As unearthed by researcher Maria Gillen, the biographer of Mrs Emily Weddall.*

Dr. Hilary Pyle's Centenary Rising Lecture on 'Cesca' at Scoil Acla, Achill Island (July 2016) in Eva O Flaherty's former Dooagh home, then and now used as an exhibition space, which held paintings by Paul Henry, Derek Hill and Marie Howet once upon a time.

Apparently, Eva's opinion was taken very seriously by her peers, and by 1918 she was up to her elbows with the Cumann's Prisoners' Sub-Committee (Food Department), following the arrest of over seventy Sinn Féin activists in the wake of the 'German Plot'. Those arrested included Countess Markievicz, Figgis, De Valera, Brian Higgins, William Cosgrave, Arthur Griffith and Sean McGarry. McGarry's wife, Tomasina Ryan, was on the Sub-Committee with Eva, as were Mimi Plunkett, Mrs Darrell Figgis (Millie), Marcella Cosgrove, J. Wyse-Power and Desmond FitzGerald's wife (and former secretary of George Bernard Shaw in London), the formidable Mabel McConnell.[4] Little wonder then that Professor F.X. Martin interviewed Eva O'Flaherty on Achill (as told to me by her young nurse there in 1963, Mary Noonan Timlin) in the early 1960s because she was a veritable gold mine of information who had been at the secret heart of nationalist Ireland for so many years. Even as late as 1948 Eva was still an important 'sound-post' because Noel Hartnett and Seán MacBride visited her home in Dooagh then (as recounted to

---

4 *As confirmed for me by Dr. Mary McAuliffe of UCD*

Since her confirmation as one of the co-founders of Cumann na mBan Professor Diarmaid Ferriter has included Eva O'Flaherty's life story in his UCD history lectures. Constitution of Cuman na mBan.

this writer by John 'Twin' McNamara) when they were founding the Clann na Poblachta party, as did Dr Noel Browne.

Dr Mark Ryan is also quite plainly a man whose life story begs many more questions, particularly when we consider those whom he called a friend, including Jeremiah O Donovan Rossa. Rossa used to stay with Ryan in his London Gower Street residence on his trans-Atlantic trips, so little wonder then that Rossa was moved to inscribe a book in Ryan's honour on the 14th March 1895 – "To Doctor Mark Ryan of Galway and of London, with the esteem of the author, O'Donovan Rossa ". Such was Ryan's precision that he appears to have included the date of his signature as well, 6pm!

The Reverend Fr. Richard Bowden conducted Rossa's Glasnevin burial in 1915 and Emily Weddall & Darrell Figgis laid (both friends of Eva O Flaherty) the first wreath from Scoil Acla on his grave. Bowden ran the Volunteer's Dependant's Fund in 1916, to which Paul Henry – probably Achill's most famous painter - via Weddall, donated a painting that year for fundraising purposes, according to researcher Maria Gillen, the biographer of Emily Weddall. In that same year, Henry did a portrait of Eva O F's brother, Arthur O'Gorman Lalor, now in Limerick, while the sketch of it is in Belfast. George Moore, for whom Mabel O Connell FitzGerald had served as a 'secretary for a time' in London, called to Emily Weddall on Achill in 1915 during one of his trips to Westport, and inscribed one of his books for her, thanking her for some fish!

Art, Achill & the painter Marie Howet

Much of Eva O'Flaherty's multi-layered story still remains to be extrapolated from the dusty vaults of history, including her pivotal role as a patroness and provider of funds and encouragement to the scores of painters who made a pilgrimage to Achill Island – and many of whom had direct links with the Tuam Art Club in the 1940s. (Alison Titley has written some great work on that topic). Some of the best known names in Irish art were personal friends of O'Flaherty –Mainie Jellett, Evie Hone, Marie Howet, Paul Henry, Derek Hill, Louis le Brocquy, and the Hamilton sisters, Eva and Letitia, all of whom will be featured in my new book on that topic, to be published in 2020, half of which will be devoted to a deep study of the life of painter Marie Howet, friend and portraitist of Eva O Flaherty, an Achill visitor for decades and the author of La Source d'Ara, published in Paris 1934. It was a limited edition of just ninety copies, which features 25 watercolours, mostly of Achill Island. Eva's home at Dooagh, which was famous for its open hearth fire piled high with the finest of island turf (according to a famous Gertrude Gaffney article about her in the Irish Independent), had a magnetic appeal for countless artists, poets

Famous Belgian Impressionist painter, Marie Howet (1897-1984), lifelong friend of Eva O'Flaherty and a visitor to Achill Island from 1929 until a few years before her death.

and writers who drifted through its doors over the years. Graham Green spent many winter nights playing cards there, and his doomed love affair on the island with the beautiful, married mother, Catherine Walston, formed the basis for his novel, The End of the Affair. So, from her Young Ireland heritage, to Paris in the late 1890s at the same times as Paul Henry and Countess Markievicz (also a fine painter) where she modelled large veiled hats for motoring cars, then on to London and the Gaelic League from 1900 onwards with the likes of Padraig ÓConaire, Sophie Bryant, Anita MacMahon, Sadhbh Trinseach (Cesca) and 'Major' Dermot Freyer, Eva O Flaherty's vivid life had all the trappings of a Hollywood mini-series and her story continues to fascinate.

SINN FEIN DELEGATES ATTEND MASS.

The four Roman Catholic members of the Sinn Fein delegation now in London—Messrs Arthur Griffith, Michael Collins, Gavan Duffy, and E. J. Duggan—attended ten o'clock mass at the Church of Corpus Christi, Maiden Lane, yesterday. They were accompanied by Messrs Art O'Brien, Desmond Fitzgerald, Sean O'Hegarty, Dr Mark Ryan, and other prominent Irishmen. The delegates were received by the Rev. Father M'Guckin, who conducted them to reserved seats. The church was filled. Mass was celebrated by the Bishop of Down and Connor (Belfast), who was assisted by the Rev. Father Thompson, C.M.

On emerging from the church they were cheered by a large crowd. Men and women pressed round Mr Collins in their efforts to shake hands, while cries of "Good Luck" and "God speed you, Michael," were frequently heard.

A snippet from The Scotsman, in which Dr. Mark Ryan is mentioned as having been in the company of Michael Collins, Arthur Griffith, Desmond FitzGerald and Art ÓBriain, at a mass in London just before the signing of the Anglo-Irish Treaty, 17 October 1921. (Courtesy Maria Gillen).

From The Liberator (March 1937), which mentions Eva as a founding member of Cumann na mBan. The article appeared in a huge spread (p.13) in the 'paper on the occasion of the 21st anniversary of the Easter Rising (Courtesy Anne Tierney, Old Tuam Society).

Mary J Murphy (mjmurphyscribe@gmail.com), a writer and mother of three, lives in Caherlistrane and is the biographer of Eva O'Flaherty. Her fourth book, ACHILL PAINTERS - featuring Alexander Williams, Paul Henry, Marie Howet, Robert Henri, Marjorie Organ, Derek Hill, Louis le Brocquy, Nano Reid, Dorothy Blackham, Stella Frost, Mabel Alleyne, Camille Souter, Maggie Morrison, Muiris MacGonigal, Stella Steyn, Maud Ball, Lillian Davidson, Estella Solomons, Eva & Letitia Hamilton, Hilda Roberts, Evie Hone, Sean Keating, Mainie Jellett, John McHugh, Charles Lamb & Sean O'Sullivan et al - will be published in 2020.

Map of Diocese of Killala

Ballycastle - Doonfeeny & Kilbride
Lacken = Lacken & Kilcummin
Killala = Killala & Templemary
Kilfian = Kilfian & Rathreagh
Knockmore = Ballinahaglish and
             Kilbelfad (or Backs)
Lahardane = Addergoole
Dromore – Kilmacshalgan

Figure 1. *Map of the Parishes of the Diocese of Killala, by Edward MacHale, Letters from the Distant Past (199*

THE FORMATION OF THE PARISHES OF KILLALA DIOCESE

Liam Alex Heffron M.A.

Cold rain slapped the windows of the stuffy overcrowded room, in the darkened upstairs of the former Welcome Inn hotel in Castlebar. They had run out of chairs, but an hour into the meeting and most were now standing, debating earnestly in low but strident tones in groups of two or three. A large map of county Mayo - projected onto a grey screen - garnered the most attention of the assembled Community Games delegates. Eyes were focussed on the borderlands between competing foes. Seated, a younger man expertly panned through the garishly coloured parish townlands, guided by the often-conflicting advice of patient - if increasingly brittle - queues of local committee representatives. The head of the County Committee stood to the side - a Mayo Community Games Bismarck in jeans - advising of the urgent need to 'get these borders agreed once and for all' and assisting the assembled parish committees swap townlands and veiled grievances with each other, to ensure everyone would leave before the cold March evening wore into a late night. As the unvolunteered representative (as is how all community officers are selected in rural Ireland) of a North Mayo parish committee, I later drove the windy, unforgiving road home, distracting my dull headache with wonder, as to how these lonely boundary streams, byroads and ditches had become the uncompromising Trumpian borders of modern rural Ireland.

All current maps of the modern parishes of Killala Diocese, appear to be based on that produced on page nine of Edward MacHale's Letters from the Distant Past - Killala Diocese in the Papal Letters and Annates, 1200-1500, published in 1991 *(Figure 1)*. Considering his authority as a senior cleric and historian of Killala Diocese, it is unsurprising that reproductions of this map, have since been used by the Catholic church, academics, the GAA, Mayo County Council, and of course the Mayo Community Games committee.

These parish boundaries are jealously guarded. In the recent past, as parochial revenues were gathered from services provided to parishioners, arguments between adjacent parish priests over the 'ownership' of small houses built into mearing ditches are found in local folklore.[1] With an overwhelmingly Catholic population, the parishes of the diocese came to be also considered as secular parishes, of which virtually everyone identified. This process was cemented by the deeply parochial GAA, who forged these units into the basic building blocks of the national sporting organisation. The author has himself witnessed heated incidents where disputes over parish boundaries have led to much table-thumping at GAA board meetings,

---

1 *Interviews by the author with natives of North Mayo, during his PhD research. A mearing is a boundary between pieces of land.*

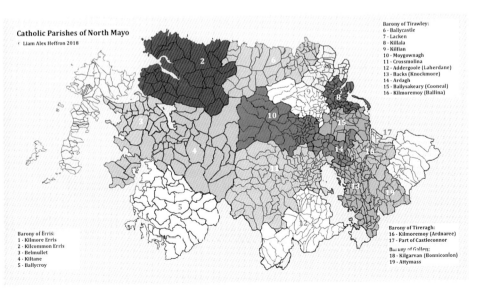

Catholic Parishes of North Mayo
© Liam Alex Heffron 2018

Barony of Tirawley:
6 - Ballycastle
7 - Lacken
8 - Killala
9 - Killian
10 - Moygownagh
11 - Crossmolina
12 - Addergoole (Laherdane)
13 - Backs (Knockmore)
14 - Ardagh
15 - Ballysakeary (Cooneal)
16 - Kilmoremoy (Ballina)

Barony of Erris:
1 - Kilmore Erris
2 - Kilcommon Erris
3 - Belmullet
4 - Kiltane
5 - Ballycroy

Barony of Tireragh:
16 - Kilmoremoy (Ardnaree)
17 - Part of Castleconnor

Barony of Gallen:
18 - Kilgarvan (Bonniconlon)
19 - Attymass

Figure 2. The parishes of North Mayo by Liam Alex Heffron (2019), including a part of Gallen barony which is not in Killala diocese. The parishes of Tireragh barony in county Sligo are not drawn.

as entitlement to play for a parish Gaelic football team is strictly based on a player's home or work base being located within its bounds.

With all that in mind, it was astonishing to learn that ALL of these maps are wrong. Compared with MacHale's *(Figure 1)* the modern map of the North Mayo parishes drawn by the present author *(Figure 2)* is quite different. Based on local history publications, interviews with natives of the area, and verified with local GAA club officers, it is intended as an accurate delineation of the present parish boundaries.[2] With MacHale's map lacking in descriptive features, it would have required a detailed examination of the 'border' townlands to realise its inaccuracies - and this was never done. It was sufficient for eyewitnesses to 'know' where the border ran between parishes, and what townlands meared it, than to accurately document it on a map. How then are the two maps so different?

According to geographer Professor Paddy J. Duffy of Maynooth University;
> 'It has been suggested that following the loss of its parochial inheritance after the reformation, and especially after the 1640s, Catholic Church administration structures had collapsed, requiring it to set about reconstructing the 'shattered parish system' in the late seventeenth century, with little reference to the medieval legacy [...] However, the eventual territorial organisation of parishes undertaken by the Catholic Church seems more conservative than radical for much of Ireland.' [3]

That said, in the diocese of Killala, it seems a combination of radical and conservative approaches were used in reforming the parish structure after the upheavals of the Plantations, several wars and the Penal Laws. This is reflected in the differences between the two maps.

Edward MacHale based his modern parish map on the surviving medieval parish structure of Killala diocese, i.e. the geographical units used by state authorities for civil administration, until the local government reforms of the later nineteenth century. These 'civil parishes' were the fossilised versions of the ecclesiastical units encountered by the seventeenth century English plantation administrators and adopted to their use, for locating and identifying forfeited townlands.

McHale's map correctly preserves the continuity of the civil parishes of Tireragh barony in Sligo, through to their catholic versions today (the Skreen and Dromard

---

2 *I am but human and thus the map may still contain some minor errors, eg. post-submission I learned that the modern Ardagh parish includes the townland of Lauvlyer (which was originally in the civil parish of Ballysakeery), where the Knox owned Netly House was situated. The map in Fig. 2 does take account of this.*
3 *Duffy PJ, 'The Shape of the Parish' in Fitzpatrick, E. and Gillespie, R. (eds.), The Parish in Medieval and Early Modern Ireland - Community, Territory and Building (Dublin, Four Courts Press 2006), pp. 36-7.*

amalgamation aside). However, the boundaries of the four 'mainland' catholic parishes of Erris - carved out of the obsolete Kilcommon civil parish - were just guesswork by him. Fortunately, more accurate parish borders can be constructed using the townland listings provided by fellow cleric and Erris historian, Sean Noone, in his book Where the Sun Sets (published in the same year as MacHale's).[4] Tirawley barony was even more complicated. Here, MacHale used amalgamations of the earlier civil parishes as his basis for the new catholic parishes. He is largely correct in the following (with the earlier civil versions in brackets); Ballycastle (Kilbride & Doonfeeny), Lacken (Lacken & Kilcummin), Killala (Killala & Templemary), and Knockmore or Backs (Ballinahaglish & Kilbelfad). He is in error with Ballina, which is actually a combination of Ardnaree and Kilmoremoy civil parishes.

It is in attempting to locate the boundaries of the interior lands west of Ballina that MacHale's map reveals its flaws. He leaves Moygownagh, Ardagh, Crossmolina and Kilfian, in their civil bounds, aside from combining Rathreagh with the latter. On the modern map (Figure 2) their boundaries appear quite different. It is clear that at some stage during the Penal decades of the late seventeenth and early eighteenth centuries, when the consolidation of the civil parishes into their larger catholic versions occurred, the local church authorities abandoned this amalgamation process. Instead the oddly shaped civil parish of Kilfian was almost completely dismembered, with the western upland portion assigned to Moygownagh. Its 'peninsula' of land in the east was divided between Moygownagh and Ardagh. The remaining townlands were then incorporated into Rathreagh, but kept its original name. In turn, Ardagh's boundary with Crossmolina moved south to the River Deel, thus creating a compact, viable unit without amalgamation. Similarly, Moygownagh's boundary with Crossmolina expanded south to take in almost all the Orme Landlord estate there.[5]

The end result of all these boundary changes were never charted or recorded, but were known by everyone living near the mearings of each parish. This 'reform' had certainly occurred or was in the process of such in Kilfian by 1704, when a Denis Kinlaghan is registered as the priest of Kilfian and Rathreagh.[6] Clearly such an amalgamation could not occur without the other boundary changes described above.

It is difficult to understand now, as to why such drastic border changes occurred

---

4 Noone, Sean, Where the Sun Sets Ballycroy, Belmullet, Kilcommon & Kiltane, County Mayo (Naas 1991). Sean Noone is also a Killala priest and local historian. Ironically, his sketch map of the Erris in the same book does not adhere to his own parish townland listings.
5 In a rare modern example of parish boundaries changing by election - the parishioners of Moygownagh voted to accede to the request by the residents of Corvoderry and Fermoyle townlands, to be received into the parish of Crossmolina which occurred on 27 May 1988 as per a plaque in St Cormac's parish church, Moygownagh.
6 MacHale, Rev Edward - The Parishes in the Diocese of Killala, Vol II (Killala 1985) pp. 66-7.

exclusively within these four 'inland' parishes - except that they surely reflected the reality of church participation in a district where the old boundaries were too contorted to be of practical benefit in consolidating church benefices. How much this displaced parishioners' routines or religious behaviour cannot now be assessed, but as Duffy notes;

> 'Stations (sometimes a response to the penal conditions in the eighteenth century where masses took place in private houses) were adopted as a mandatory practice which helped to consolidate the coherence of parish identity.' [7]

Such measures coupled with the deep social disruptions of post-plantation land ownership and war, accentuated by state sponsored sectarianism, may have overridden people's resistance to change and attachment to a 'territorial community, territorial allegiance and identity. [whereas now] modern changes in parishes are also greatly resented and seldom fully implemented.' [8]

Thomas McDonnell, a former Catholic Bishop of Killala, attempted in 1976 to understand how the parishes of the diocese originated.[9] In his The Diocese of Killala, from its institution to the end of penal times, he identified a 1306 taxation list of churches in Killala Diocese as a list of parish churches. 'Parishes are said by historians to have been laid out in the thirteenth century", McDonnell baldly stated, which to him confirmed that this early list is one of parish churches and identified with the modern catholic parishes in the diocese. He also believed that this medieval parish formation was planned, similar to the division of (mainland) Erris into modern catholic parishes during the nineteenth century;

> 'Firstly, we can safely assume that in Erris at this time it was made by the Bishop in consultation with the priests and people concerned. The State authorities would have entered only to take cognisance of it afterwards. The considerations acting upon were obvious (1) the location of existing churches and Mass-houses, (2) traditional orientations of areas towards them arising from the geography of the area and the distribution of population, (3) the need to provide an area big enough to support at least one priest. With these in mind the area would have fallen into four natural units and it appears that these were set up as the four parishes.'[10]

However, this is but complete guesswork on McDonnell's part. His modern theory is of little use in understanding how a thirteenth century parish could have been

---

7 *Duffy, 'The Shape of the Parish', p. 36. The 'Mass Stations' tradition continued down to relatively recent times in North Mayo, where groups of townlands known 'station areas', rotated a bi-annual mass held in each consecutive house, usually followed with a celebratory meal for the priest, family and neighbours.*
8 *Ibid p. 33.*
9 *McDonnell, Rev Thomas, The Diocese of Killala, from its institution to the end of penal times (Ballina 1976), pp. 31-37.*
10 *Ibid, p. 35.*

formed. He later admits that several Tirawley parishes 'have their churches in the very extremity of their parishes and the very odd shapes of Kilfian and Ardagh could not possibly represent the clientele of these churches'.[11] His solution was to have the (anonymous) authorities initially proceed around the perimeter of the diocese, forming parishes for viable units of population. This left a long irregular strip left in the centre, which was 'then assigned to Kilfian and Ardagh churches'.[12] Unfortunately, McDonnell provides no proof for any of this and actually ends his chapter with:

> 'It is held that in some other areas of Ireland the parishes corresponded to the 'fees' of the Anglo-Norman settlers but there seems to be no evidence that this was, or was not, so in Killala. The big number of small parishes in Tirawley reflects Anglo-Norman influence; it is said that this was a feature of areas under their control.' [13]

Why the Bishop thought his diocese did not owe its parish formation to the Anglo-Normans is not clear, but it is with these thirteenth century invaders of North Connacht that the solution may be found.

Historian Paul MacCotter has pioneered a fascinating and forensic analysis of early Gaelic medieval records and their later Anglo-Norman counterparts, in his determination to understand the roles of the Norman Manor, Gaelic (late) Tùath and how they both affected parish formation.[14] According to MacCotter;

> 'In the matter of parish boundaries, we must note that the present (civil) parish boundary structure was first recorded in the early nineteenth century. The Down Survey of 1654-56 is the only significant prior mapping of parish boundaries. It records most such boundaries and shows them to be similar to those mapped in the nineteenth century.'[15]

Thus, these English maps charting (i.e. noting 'down') the forced transfer of lands from Catholic to Protestant ownership in the seventeenth century plantations, confirmed that the civil parish boundaries remained unchanged with the old medieval parishes being adopted for official use as civilian geographical locators (and thus known as civil parishes thereafter).

---

11 Ibid.
12 Ibid, p. 36.
13 Ibid, p. 37.
14 MacCotter, Paul – 'Tùath, Manor and Parish- Kingdom of Fir Maige, Cantred of Fermoy' in Peritia - Journal of the Medieval Academy of Ireland, (2011) Vol 23-24, pp. 224-274. MacCotter uses 'late Tùath' of pre-Norman Ireland to distinguish it from the local kingdoms of early Medieval Ireland (and popular history!). 'The [late] tùath may be thought of as the earliest manifestation of the local community, best represented in more recent times by the secular elements of the concept of the rural parish.' (p. 248).
15 Ibid p. 230. An examination of the Mayo books of Survey and Distribution revealed the Civil Parishes listed there are the same found in the 19th century Ordnance Survey records for North Mayo, on identified townland basis. Space restriction does not allow the results to be presented here.

But where did these medieval parishes have their genesis? In his research into the Fermoy district of Cork, MacCotter found a continuity of medieval parishes down to the nineteenth century.

' [...] the modern parish structure, with few exceptions, is largely that of the 1590s, but that some differences are indicated by earlier records, showing a significant level of parish amalgamation and a lesser level of boundary alteration during the fourteenth and fifteenth centuries. Where parish amalgamations occur these involve mostly the smallest parishes, and such a process may well be the result of the decades-long period of marked population decline beginning in the middle of the fourteenth century. As to actual parish boundary changes, these are much less common.'[16]

A similar examination of the seventeenth century land records for Killala diocese, shows this to be true for the civil parishes therein. Edward MacHale mentions a number of 'vicarages' in the Papal letters exchanged with Killala Diocese during the fourteenth and fifteenth centuries, of which some had ceased to exist by the time of the plantation documents.[17] These vicarages supported a priest administering to his congregation, and were attached to the church of the same name.[18] Thus, they may be considered as being the one and the same entity, found in the later documents as parishes. The 'extinct' vicarages included; 'Errew' (now in Crossmolina) mentioned in 1459, 1460, 1469, 1471; 'Rosserk' (now in Ballysakeery) is mentioned in 1434, 1455 and 1458; and 'Bothmoryn and Glyn' - listed in the 1306 taxation list of churches above - which MacHale identifies as the vicarage of Bofeenaun, now in Addergoole. He admits that the latter vicarage was ' [...] perhaps a parish, which became amalgamated later because of its size.' [19] These medieval amalgamations can explain why Crossmolina and Addergoole were so large in geographical extent and curiously, perhaps also as to why these two civil parishes - along with Ballysakeery - are the only ones in Tirawley not to amalgamate or increase their boundaries during the Penal times.

As for the remaining vicarages (aka parishes), which re-emerged in the English land confiscation documents of the mid-seventeenth century, many of the smaller units were later merged into church of Ireland 'unions', for better management of clergy (and a smaller protestant congregation). The civil parishes continued to be used for official state purposes until late into the nineteenth century, to be finally

16 Ibid, pp. 230-1.
17 MacHale, Mgr. Edward, Letters from the Distant Past - Killala Diocese in the Papal Letters and Annates, 1200-1500, (Ballina 1991) p. 17. 'The Calendars of Papal Registers, or Papal Letters as they are usually called, give us copies of correspondence with the Holy See concerning questions of government and administration from the different dioceses and the decisions taken in their regard.' as per MacHale.
18 Ibid. p. 47. I have annotated MacHale's detailed explanation of the term.
19 Ibid, p. 237.

replaced by what became District Electoral Divisions (or DEDs), several of which make up larger Electoral Areas.

It should also be noted that the barony of Erris was assessed as one single entity in the 1306 taxation list and was only divided into the civil parishes of Kilmore Erris (the peninsula) and the sprawling Kilcommon Erris by the seventeenth century. The later civil parish was then subdivided into its four catholic inheritors in the nineteenth century, which McDonnell alluded to above.

As MacCotter has argued in Fermoy, we can trace parish formation there even further back to the twelfth and thirteenth centuries, with the arrival of the Anglo-Normans.[20]

Such was the close relationship between manors/knights' fees and parishes in the Anglo-Norman domain that a manor was held in law to carry automatically the right of advowson (that is, to 'present' the priest). Even where no explicit statement describing a fee as a 'manor' exists, where one finds the local (land)lord possessing or claiming such a right one can be certain that this indicates that the parish in question has a parallel manor, and that the manor was established before the parish.' [21]

We can see the same circumstances in Killala diocese, as the Anglo-Normans were settled in North Mayo from at least the mid-thirteenth century (as evidenced by a deed of 1244, signed by Bishop of Killala and several Anglo-Norman nobles).[22] The initial large grants of territory by regional lords such as Richard deBurgo to lesser nobles, then saw these 'manors' broken up into sub-manors in a process known as sub-infeudation, which was eventually outlawed by the Quia Emptores statute in 1290.[23] Thus, the formation of parishes must have taken place before this. The small medieval parishes found in the barony of Tirawley likely reflect the many smaller sub-manors of lesser Norman nobles, which developed in tandem.

But there is ample evidence in both Fermoy and Killala of an even earlier pre-Norman system of pastoral organisation. As per MacCotter, this Gaelic system was based on the 'late tùath' or local territory of a Gaelic chief, who was deposed by the invading Anglo-Normans.[24]

---

20 MacCotter, 'Tùath, Manor and Parish', pp. 224-274.
21 Ibid, p. 229.
22 M6807, (Box 5, no. 1) Palmer Papers as held in the National Archives, but now missing.
23 Quia Emptores is a statute passed in the reign of Edward I of England in 1290 that prevented tenants from alienating their lands to others by subinfeudation (carving out new and distinct tenures in their turn by sub-letting), instead requiring all tenants who wished to alienate their land to do so by substitution (i.e. effectively swapping their tenures).
24 MacCotter, 'Tùath, Manor and Parish', pp. 229-30, 248.

'[...] significant continuity between pre- and post-Invasion estate boundaries [suggesting] in most cases the process of manor creation took some account of tùath boundaries.'

He is further of the opinion that these,

> 'late-tùath may well have been in existence as early as the period of legal codification in the seventh and eighth centuries.' [25]

These larger 'late-tùath' territories, were often granted in whole to the new invaders,[26] but became fragmented in Tirawley barony as the Normans carved it up into their own smaller lordships. However, the religious units based on the 'late-tùath' survived into late medieval times as 'rectories', whose income became fiercely contested in the aforementioned Papal Letters. Often, an heir to the original grantee of a 'late-tùath', would claim the right of presentation to churches now found within the former territory, despite that grant having been since broken up among a series of manors and sub-manors, each having their own vicarage. A clue as to why this especially happened in Tirawley is revealed by the late nineteenth century Mayo antiquarian and historian, Hubert Knox;

> 'English settlers fought against each other in Tirawley, at Kilroe near Killala, in 1281. The Justiciary Rolls and the Annals of Loch Cé mention the battle, but not its immediate cause, which may have grown out of the claims of Adam Cusack and William Barrett of Bac and Glen to the land of Bredagh, under early deBurgo grants which gave rise to litigation in 1253.' [27]

The churches of Moygownagh and Kilfian are found in the Papal Letters as located within the rectory of Bredagh. Thus, as Knox states, a series of conflicting grants of land led to competing claims, among several minor Anglo-Norman families. This in turn resulted in a division of territories into smaller units in an effort to satisfy all the parties concerned. This is clear from the details of the thirteenth century efforts of William Barrett to hold onto Bredagh, after he ejected a former Anglo-Norman occupier, by giving parts of it to his lord Richard deBurgo, in order to hold the remainder.[28]

It was the Penal times stress that forced the Catholic diocese to create new viable parishes through combinations of; radical division of some of the older civil parishes; with enlargement and amalgamation of others, as and where it suited. By tracing the origins of Killala parishes back to the Anglo-Norman manors of the thirteenth century, we find they took shape from efforts to stave off civil war among these invaders. Alleged allies swapped townland ownership in previously

---

25 *Ibid, p. 248.*
26 *Ibid, p. 248.*
27 *Knox, Hubert Thomas, The history of the county of Mayo to the close of the sixteenth century (Dublin 1908), p.121.*
28 *Ibid, pp. 291-292.*

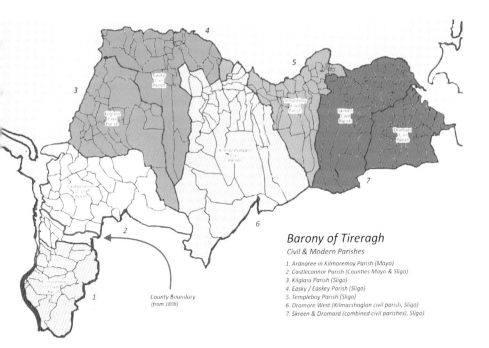

Figure 3: *Barony of Tireragh – Civil & Modern Parishes.*

Barony of Tireragh
Civil & Modern Parishes

1. Ardnaree in Kilmoremoy Parish (Mayo)
2. Castleconnor Parish (Counties Mayo & Sligo)
3. Kilglass Parish (Sligo)
4. Easky / Easkey Parish (Sligo)
5. Templeboy Parish (Sligo)
6. Dromore West (Kilmacshaglan civil parish), Sligo)
7. Skreen & Dromard (combined civil parishes), Sligo)

County Boundary
(from 1898)

Gaelic territories to prevent open warfare among them. This had eerie echoes in that tense Castlebar hotel room in a few weeks ago. Parish boundaries had held their vitality for over a thousand years and would continue to, for another night at least!

(see www.timeteam.ie for detailed maps and more information).

Bibliography

Duffy PJ, 'The Shape of the Parish' in Fitzpatrick, E. and Gillespie, R. (eds.), *The Parish in Medieval and Early Modern Ireland - Community, Territory and Building* (Dublin, Four Courts Press 2006).

Knox, Hubert Thomas, *The history of the county of Mayo to the close of the sixteenth century* (Dublin 1908).

MacCotter, Paul, 'Tùath, Manor and Parish- Kingdom of Fir Maige, Cantred of Fermoy' in *Peritia - Journal of the Medieval Academy of Ireland*, Vol. 22-23 (2011).

MacHale, Mgr. Edward, *Letters from the Distant Past - Killala Diocese in the Papal Letters and Annates, 1200-1500* (Ballina 1991).

MacHale, Rev Edward - *The Parishes in the Diocese of Killala, Vol II* (Killala 1985).

McDonnell, Rev Thomas, *The Diocese of Killala, from its institution to the end of penal times* (Ballina 1976).

Noone, Sean, *Where the Sun Sets Ballycroy, Belmullet, Kilcommon & Kiltane, County Mayo* (Naas 1991).

Simington Robert C, *Books of survey and distribution, County of Mayo* (Dublin : Stationery Office 1956).

Primary sources. National Archives (Dublin)

M6807, (Box 5, no. 1) *A seventeenth century Palmer lease in the as held in the National Archives, but now missing. This document recited an older charter between the bishop of Killala and a Laurence and Christian Magorday, and signed by several Anglo-Norman nobles including a William Barrett. The date was transcribed as 7 September MCCXLIII.*

Ordnance Survey Field Name Books, Mayo (1838).

Liam Alex Heffron M.A. is an Entrepreneur, Actor and Historian. He published 'No Revolution - Igniting war in North Mayo, 1917-1923' (Mayo County Library, 2018). He is Founder and Director of the award-winning ANSEO project - to digitally preserve the historical records of Irish national schools. He is teaching history at NUI Galway. His PhD is titled, 'The revolutionary intersection of land hunger, social justice impulse, and memory in the rural west of Ireland, 1918-1923'. He still plays junior club football in his native Mayo. www.liamalexheffron.com and www.anseo.ie

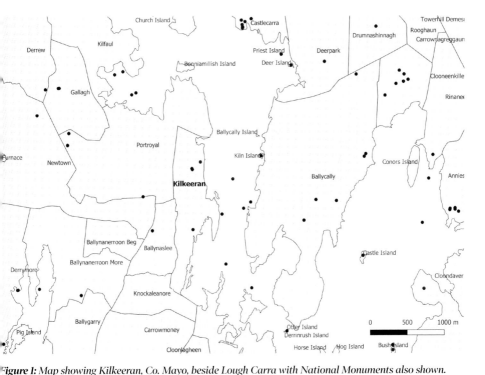

Figure I: *Map showing Kilkeeran, Co. Mayo, beside Lough Carra with National Monuments also shown.*

THE MEDIEVAL CHURCHES
OF KILKEERAN, CO. MAYO

Dr Yvonne McDermott

This article considers the architecture of three stone churches of medieval date at Kil-keeran, Co. Mayo. Their location and the surviving structural evidence will be consid-ered to see what insights may be gleaned as to the former appearance of these buildings. The townland of Kilkeeran will be introduced briefly in the following discussion and some consideration will be given to St Ciarán, after whom this area is named.

The townland of Kilkeeran is located on the western shore of Lough Carra (Fig-ure 1) and was recorded as being of 373 acres, 2 roods and 24 perches in extent in Griffith's Valuation in the nineteenth century. It is in the barony of Carra and is one of 42 townlands in the civil parish of Ballyovey (MacGabhann 2014, 144).[1] The

---

[1] *The Catholic parish structure in Ireland was reconstituted in the late seventeenth century (Duffy 2005, 6). In attempting to recover the medieval parishes, it can be useful to look at the civil parishes, a divi-sion frequently used for government purposes in the nineteenth century.*

place name 'Kilkeeran', a transliteration of the Irish 'Cill Chiarán', has been rendered in many different spelling variants and sometimes in the early modern period the element 'oughter' or variations on it were appended to the name (MacGabhann 2014 186). This derives from 'uachtar', meaning upper.

As discussed below, Ciarán was a popular saint's name in early medieval Ireland This perhaps also helps explain the popularity of Kilkeeran as a place name. According to the General Alphabetical Index of Townlands and Towns, Parishes and Baronies in Ireland (Anon. 1861, 562) there are three other townlands of this name in Mayo, two in the barony of Kilmaine and one in the barony of Costello. In addition, townlands called Kilkeeran were recorded in 1851 in King's County (Offaly) and Meath. Furthermore, three townlands called Kilkieran (note the slight variation in spelling) were recorded in Clare, Galway and Kilkenny (Anon. 1861, 562).

The Ordnance Survey Letters for County Mayo, originally compiled in 1838, record the ruins of three churches in Kilkeeran, noting that they are 'much destroyed' (Herity 2009, 205). The first edition Ordnance Survey map of the same year positions one church very close to the village of Kilkeeran, towards the centre of this long narrow townland. The field in which it is located is known locally as 'Tempaleem' (Lavelle 1994, 87). Two more churches are located towards the northern end of the townland, where is it bounded by Portroyal on its north and west sides. The more southerly of these two churches is located within a graveyard. Again all three are recorded as being in ruins. Of the three churches, the example in the graveyard is by far the best preserved of the three. Although a ruin, the surviving remains are in a reasonable state, providing more insights than those of the other two churches, which survive in a much more fragmentary condition.

St Ciarán

The townland and at least one of the churches in it are dedicated to St Ciarán Early medieval sources record 26 saints of this name in Ireland (MacGabhann 2014 187), of whom two are particularly well known. Saints at this time achieved such status through popular acclaim, rather than through the official canonisation procedures followed today. In the medieval period, saints were holy people who could perform miracles, in life and after death, through God's grace (Downham 2018 122).

St Ciarán the elder (fl. 450-500) (Johnston 2008, online), also called Ciarán of Saighir (Seirkieran, about 8km from Birr, Co. Offaly), became patron saint of the diocese of Ossory (Breen 2009, 513). He is considered to be one of Ireland's pilgrim saints and the Martyrology of Óengus describes him as 'city-possessing Ciarán the hostful of Saighir' and 'Poor Ciarán, a noble coarb, senior of the saints, a jewel in rank' (Stokes 1905, 80).

Figure 2: *Cross of the Scriptures (replica) at Clonmacnoise with the cathedral in the background.*

St Ciarán of Clonmacnoise (c. 515-548/9)[2] (Stalmans & Charles-Edwards 2007, online) is the most celebrated of the saints of that name, with his feast day falling on 9th September (Farmer 2003, 106-7).[3] Three 'Lives' of the saint survive. These attest that he studied with St Finian of Clonard and St Enda of Aran, and that he established a monastery at Clonmacnoise (*Figure 2*) on the Shannon a year before his death (Stalmans & Charles-Edwards 2007, online). Like many of his contemporaries, St Ciarán has numerous legends associated with him. A particularly striking example is the story that the saints of Ireland were so jealous of him that, with the exception of St Columcille, they prayed and fasted that he would die young (Farmer 203, 107; Ó hÓgáin 2006, 85). His direct cause of death was remembered as being plague (Bhreathnach 2014, 184).[4] The names of both saints are anglicised as Kieran. It is not clear which, if either, of these two saints has an association with Kilkeeran near Lough Carra.

The churches

Of the three churches in the townland of Kilkeeran, two churches (A & C, see Table 1 for corresponding details) are of early medieval date, while the third (Church B) is of high to late medieval date. The ruins of the two early medieval churches are fairly fragmentary. It is possible to reconstruct the footprint of both churches but there is less evidence concerning the walls and roof. Church B offers more extant evidence today and it is possible to gain a much greater insight into the former appearance of this building than is the case with the other two churches.

Kilkeeran churches, from north to south					
	National Monument No.	Location	Dimensions	Name	Note
A	MA099-026----	Towards north of townland	14.8m x 7.7m	Unknown	North church
B	MA099-025001-	In graveyard (MA099-025002-)	15.6m x 7.7m	Ballyovey Parish Church	Parish church
C	MA109-006----	In 'Teampaleem', field beside village	16m x 7.8m	St Kieran's Church	South church

Table 1: The medieval churches of Kilkeeran, Co. Mayo.

In studying the two early medieval churches of Kilkeeran, it proved worthwhile to consult GH Kinahan's (1868b, 131-8) study of the cyclopean churches of Loughs Carra, Mask and Corrib. Leaving aside for a moment the accuracy or applicability of the term 'cyclopean' to which we will return, the value of this study lies in part in its age, reflecting a time when these churches survived in a somewhat better state than they do today. Nonetheless, Kinahan (1868a, 76) observes that 'the present generation are fast destroying what remains' of these early churches.

---

2 These dates fit with the tradition that St Ciarán was aged 33 at the time of his death, the same age at which Jesus was crucified (Ó hÓgáin 2006, 85).
3 His mother Dar Erca was believed to be St Patrick's sister but this assertion is dismissed by Stalmans & Charles-Edwards (2007, online) as having a familiar ring of Patrician propaganda about it.
4 A number of other significant monastic founders are also recorded as dying in 549, including Finian of Clonard and Column of Inishcealtra (Bhreathnach 2014, 185).

Figure 3: *Teampall Bheanáin on Inishmore, Aran Islands. Includes many of the features common to early medieval Irish churches but with an unusual north-south alignment.*

Churches in medieval Ireland were built of wood and stone, in addition to other materials. The former lies beyond the scope of this study, although it is worth reflecting on the possibility that the surviving early medieval churches at Kilkeeran may once also have been accompanied by other structures built of more ephemeral materials. Ó Carragáin's (2010) Churches in Early Medieval Ireland: Architecture, Ritual and Memory offers a detailed account of the construction of churches of materials other than stone, based on archaeological and documentary evidence. The side walls of the churches tended to not be particularly tall but the gable ends could be of more impressive height, partly owing to the steep pitch (c. 60 degrees) of many early medieval church roofs, a design necessitating a high gable (Leask 1955, 53). In their simplest form, doorways could be spanned by a single lintel. Typically, the jambs tend to incline slightly towards each other (Leask 1955, 56). Windows tended to be few in number and small in size, most commonly located in the east wall; there are sometimes also south-facing examples (Leask 1955, 58) *(Figure 3)*.

The blame for the structural decline of these 'cyclopean' churches around the western lakes is laid by Kinahan (1868a, 76) at the feet of 'the Danes', 'mercenary soldiers of the DeBurgos and other Anglo-Norman conquerors'. The usual suspects, Elizabeth I and Cromwell, don't receive a mention on this occasion.

Early medieval Irish churches of stone tended to be laid out according to a consistent set of principles. These simple structures were usually small in size and unicameral, or single chambered, with no division between nave and chancel. Local stone tended to be used in construction, not least because this helped limit the cost of the structure as moving stone could quickly become an expensive undertaking. Lough Carra and the area to the west of it lie on a bed of Carboniferous limestone that was formed about 350 million years ago (Huxley & Huxley 2015, 21).

Cyclopean masonry is a type found in antiquity (Stevens Curl 2000, 188). Although the term was once widely used in relation to early medieval churches in Ireland, it has fallen out of favour in some quarters or at least been subject to more critical discussion. Stevens Curl (2000, 188) defines cyclopean[5] masonry as being 'composed of irregularly shaped very large blocks, sometimes approximating to polygons, dressed sufficiently for them to fit tightly together without mortar'. Ó Carragáin (2005, 100) contends that the Irish examples don't entirely fit this description as they are mortared. Nonetheless, he rejects calls to abandon the term entirely in discussions relating to Irish architecture, suggesting it has a value in describing churches that have some cyclopean characteristics. Leask (1955, 53) disputes the use of the term with reference to Ireland, arguing that the Irish work, 'while less gigantic, is more accomplished'.

The cyclopean or massive nature of this masonry is often an illusion, consisting of large but thin sheets of stone, placed on their edge, obscuring a rubble fill at the core of the wall (Stalley 2005, 731). Such material would have been readily available in the limestone areas of the west where many 'cyclopean' churches occur. Leask (1955, 51) remarks that through this method 'the appearance rather than the fact of great massiveness' was obtained. This may help explain how at least some of these apparently massive stones were moved into place. Ó Carragáin (2010, 159) refutes Leask's (1955, 51-3) suggestion that cyclopean blocks were a response to the local environment, used to save mortar, a theory negated by the use of mortar in the buildings' rubble cores. Instead, he attributes the builders' use of such large stones to a desire to achieve a monumental quality in their buildings. Early medieval churches in Ireland were typically of modest proportions but in a land of small churches, monumentality could be achieved

---

5 *The most well-known meaning of the term cyclopean is of course in the following sense 'belonging to or resembling the Cyclops; monstrous, gigantic, huge; single, or large and round, like the eye of one of the Cyclops' (OED, 2019). The emphasis on massiveness is carried into the architectural definition.*

through materials rather than overall scale. It is also worth considering whether such stones were intended to be seen in the final design. If the building was whitewashed, the outline of the masonry would have remained visible when the building was complete. The buildings could have been rendered externally, although internal render may have been more common (Ó Carragáin 2010, 160-1). The great size of stones used, or appearance of such, appears to have left an impression on folklore. The Venerable Bede, in writing of St Cuthbert's construction of a hermitage on Lindisfarne, noted the great size of the stones used, 'so large that four men could hardly have lifted them', but they were put in place by Cuthbert 'with angels helping him' (Giles 1843, 37). It is perhaps not a surprise that over time the construction of a cyclopean church came to be seen as indicative of the founders saint's miracle-working powers, as was the case in Fore, Co. Westmeath, where a great lintel was said to have been moved into place by St Feichin (Ó Carragáin 2010, 159).

Ó Carragáin (2005, 110-120) provides a detailed analysis of the characteristics of masonry in pre-Romanesque Irish churches, including Kilkeeran. The portion relating to Kilkeeran is summarised in Table 2. It indicates the absence of joggle joints but the presence of spalls (Ó Carragáin 2005, 117). The spaces between large blocks of stone could be filled with smaller stones, called spalls (Leask 1955, 53). The use of such space fillers is not, strictly speaking, cyclopean, as this style of masonry relied on large blocks of stone that fitted together (Ó Carragáin 2010, 117). As discussed earlier, we need not concern ourselves with the application of a strict definition of cyclopean masonry to these churches. Joggle joints are masonry joints consisting of a projection on one piece that fits in a notch in another (Stevens Curl 2000, 349). They are used to prevent sliding.

Kilkeeran	
Stone used	Limestone
Coursing	Coursed
Block size range	Medium to large
On edge	A few
Shape	Some irregular
Fitting	Quite good
Joggle joints	No
Spalls	Quite a few
Visible mortar	None visible

Table 2: Summary of information relating to Kilkeeran from Ó Carragáin (2005, 110-120).

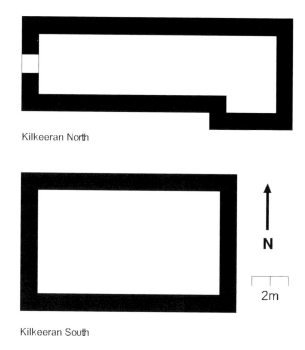

Kilkeeran North

N

2m

Kilkeeran South

Figure 4: *Floor plans of the two early medieval churches in Kilkeeran townland.*

There are challenges in dating buildings of this type as masonry styles are not necessarily indicative of a particular date. The absence of surviving window openings also adds to the challenge of establishing the age of the buildings as these can prove useful in establishing a date range.

In his nineteenth-century study of cyclopean churches, Kinahan (1868b, 137) provides a description of both of the early churches at Kilkeeran, including dimensions. These facilitate the creation of floor plans showing the footprint of both buildings *(Figure 4)*. He observes that the southern church was 'much dilapidated' with only parts of the south-east and north walls surviving *(Figure 5)*. Its close proximity to the village and lack of mortar did not assist its survival as Kinahan (1868b, 137) records that much of the rest of the walls were pulled down to build houses in the nearby village. The reuse of masonry from the churches for new purposes to some extent reflects the medieval practice of reusing building materials known as 'spolia' (Ó Carragáin 2010, 156). Lives of the Irish saints indicate there was a symbolic element to this practice (Ó Carragáin 2010, 156); the modern motive may relate more to convenience. The northern church lacks any tradition, not even a dedication is known. Perhaps because of its less populous location it survived in a better state to Kinahan's time *(Figure 6)*. Four walls remained and one side of a doorway survived in the west wall *(Figure 7)* (Kinahan 1868, 137).

Figure 5: *Masonry from the southern church beside the village of Kilkeeran.*

Figure 6: *Masonry at Kilkeeran north. The two large upright stones are of the type used in early medieval church construction.*

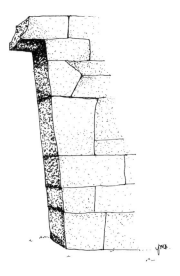

Figure 7: Doorway of the north church in Kilkeeran. Based on a drawing in Kinahan (1868).

Parish church

The last of the three medieval churches of Kilkeeran townland to be considered here is the medieval parish church, located within a cemetery that remains in use today. The parish name, Ballyovey, is associated with this church. The church located within the cemetery in Kilkeeran townland is of a basic rectangular plan (Figure 8), with a doorway surmounted by a simple, pointed arch in the west wall and a twin-light cusped tracery window in the east wall. There is a second doorway in the south wall, slightly to the west of centre, with a single-light pointed window towards the east end of the same wall. The two end walls survive reasonably intact; with only the west wall lacking its apex. The lateral walls have not survived so well. Both are missing a portion in the centre. The north wall is lacking the largest proportion of its original material.

Figure 8: Plan of Ballyovey parish church, located in the townland of Kilkeeran

Knox (1904, 222) contends that formerly the parish of Ballyovey was named Bal-lynegarry. This name now applies to a townland located at the northern end of Lough Mask (about 1km from Kilkeeran). He does not make his rationale for this entirely clear: 'I take it to be a name used for the whole parish for some reason' (Knox 1904, 222). Supporting Knox's (1904, 222) assertion, the editor of the Cal-endar of Papal Registers (Vol. XII) lists Ballygarry (and variants) as the former name for Ballyovey parish (Twemlow, 1933, 838-53). However, Nicholls (1971, 71-2) disputes this association, suggesting the names of its holders and benefices imply a connection with Clanmorris. Furthermore, MacGabhann (2014, 145), in his vast and authoritative study of places names in Mayo, notes that Knox was mistaken in reading of the sources.[6]

MacGabhann (2014, 143-4) translates Baile Óbha (Ballyovey) as 'townland of Óbha (lumpy place)'. He notes some disagreement in the literature as to whether Óbha is a territorial name or a descriptive term referring to a lumpy, bumpy place or a knot in a tree. 'Fayte' (from Faiche, a green) may be an early name used for this place (MacGabhann 2014, 145). It is mentioned in an ecclesiastical taxation of c. 1307 with a value of 20s associated with the church, which is located in the deancry of Mayo (Sweetman & Handcock 1896, 232). It also records the tithes levied. The place names 'Ome' and 'Homy' have also been tentatively associated with Ballyo-vey (MacGabhann 2014, 143). Both occur in the Obligationes pro Annatis Provin-ciae Tuamensis or 'annates' of the ecclesiastical province of Tuam (Anon. 1963, 56-117).[7] The annates of 1430 record Thoma Oranayn as vicar of the parish of 'Ome' in the diocese of Tuam (Anon. 1963, 66). In 1471 the place name 'Homy' is used (Anon. 1963, 208). The rendering of place names in these documents is often challenging; the lack of standardised spelling making them very obscure at times. While some annates were edited for publication with explanatory footnotes, for example Egan and Costello's (1958, 52-74) edition of the Clonfert annates, others, including Tuam, were published as transcriptions of the Latin text.[8]

As part of the Gregorian Reform of the Irish Church in the twelfth century, the Church in Ireland moved from a predominantly monastic form of organisation to a 'hierarchical and territorial church' (Ní Ghabhláin 1996, 37). This saw the estab-lishment of dioceses, gradually followed by parishes.

While much progress has been made on the study of parish churches in Ireland, notably FitzPatrick and Gillespie's (2005) The Parish in Medieval and Early Medi-eval Ireland, we still lack a detailed study of the type produced by Fawcett (2002)

6 *'Bhí dul amú ar Knox faoi úsáid Ballingarry sna foinsí'* (MacGabhann 2014, 145).
7 *Annates were a papally-imposed tax on minor benefices in Ireland (Connolly 2002, 40), introduced in the early fourteenth century but not enforced until the fifteenth century (O'Connell & Costello 1958, 1).*
8 *See MacGabhann (2014, 143-5) for a more detailed treatment of the place name Ballyovey and its use from the medieval period onwards.*

Figure 9: *West doorway of Ballyovey parish church.*

on Scottish churches. A number of local studies on parish churches in Ireland have been published. Prominent amongst these is Ní Ghabhláin's (1995, 61-84; 1996, 37-61) studies of the diocese of Kilfenora.

FitzPatrick (2005, 62-3), in her discussion of the material remains of the parish church, defines parochial status as being indicated by the presence of a baptismal font and a fenced graveyard. A baptismal font was not identified at Kilkeeran during the current study but there is an enclosure around the site containing the church and graveyard. FitzPatrick (2005, 63-4) also identifies a series of other items that may hint at parish status but which are also associated with chapels. The church in Kilkeeran features a number of these elements. It consists of a clearly defined liturgical space, although there is no surviving indication of where the division between nave and chancel was located, if such a division ever existed. This is partly due to the ruinous state of the lateral walls around the central portion of the church. The church is located within a cemetery and there are a number of modern burial markers within the church itself. There is no surviving evidence for the kinds of aumbries that often occur near the eastern end of churches, nor for a piscina or a stoup. The

Figure 10: *Interior of the west wall of Ballyovey parish church. Note the numbered stones to the left of the doorway.*

Sites and Monuments Records do not record any archaeological features other than the church and the graveyard in the vicinity; indeed the two early medieval churches discussed above are the only two other entries for the townland of Kilkeeran.

The dimensions of the church at Kilkeeran are consistent with those recorded for parish churches by Ní Ghabhláin (1995, 68) in her study of the churches of the diocese of Kilfenora, Co. Clare. She records a number of chapels but the maximum length of each of these is below 10m.9 Ní Ghabhláin (1995, 71) discuses a range of chapel types that occur in Kilfenora diocese. The largest of these were chapels of ease, located in remote areas of large parishes. No baptismal fonts or burial grounds occurred at such sites, in contrast to Kilkeeran which has a graveyard, a feature that supports parish church status.

In terms of dating buildings, it is worth examining styles of windows and doorways when dating medieval churches. However, these are not necessarily indicative of the date of the church as such features can be later insertions. Ní Ghabhláin (1995, 80) reports that a number of churches in the diocese of Kilfenora experienced considerable refurbishment in the fifteenth and sixteenth centuries. This could be a useful alternative to constructing new churches and could allow the continuity with the past that was often prized in medieval building.

The west doorway of the church, the main portal used by the congregation to access the structure, features a simple pointed Gothic arch (*Figure 9*). Some of the arch stones are chamfered, while others are not, suggesting that not all of the stones used are original to this location. In addition, a number of stones in this doorway are clearly modern insertions, put in situ during conservation works. There are three such stones along the southern jamb of the exterior of the door and another lies to the right of the centre of the arch. They lack the weathering of their neighbouring stones and are somewhat different in colour. The interior view of the western wall features a series of numbered stones, mostly to the left of the doorway, another sign of modern conservation work (*Figure 10*).

The window in the southern wall of the church is a pointed, narrow opening, similar to a lancet but shorter (*Figure 11*). On the inside, above the sill, there is a second narrower sill, perhaps suggesting that the height of the window was shortened at some point (although it is worth noting that the east window has the same feature). The external view of the window shows that the stone across the base of the opening is a modern insertion. The surround of the window opening is chamfered and a matching cutaway has been taken from the inserted stone. The window lacks the hood-moulding typical of late medieval Gothic windows in Ireland, perhaps an indication of high medieval date.

---

9 *She also notes that the area of the nave reflects the size of the community served (Ní Ghabhláin 1995, 67). However, it has not proved possible to identify where the nave and chancel meet at Kilkeeran, so we lack this insight into congregation size.*

The east window is the crowning glory of any church. The example at Kilkeeran lacks its central mullion and some of the tracery from its upper portion *(Figure 12)*. Nonetheless, sufficient evidence survives to give us an indication of how this window might once have looked. It is surmounted by a hood-moulding with its ends terminating in points. The heavily moulded nature of the mullion and its surviving tracery speak to the sophistication of this window. It had only two lights and it was not large by the standards of the time. It is nonetheless in keeping with the proportions of the church overall *(Figure 13)*. It is noteworthy that this window features cusped tracery, a useful chronological indicator. It is a characteristic of the Late Irish Gothic style but fell out of favour in the late fifteenth century (McNeill 2006, 224) with less ornamented styles being preferred. A similar fashion was evident in contemporary France and Scotland (McNeill 2006, 222). The window features 'subsidiary head pieces' (Mooney 1956, 139) below the lowest section of interlace. It is not possible to tell from the surviving portions whether these were round (as at Moyne friary) or pointed (as at Ross Errilly).

Conclusion

Despite limited documentary evidence, it is possible to glean some insights into the medieval heritage of Kilkeeran. Our understanding of the fragmentary remains of the early medieval churches is helped by the existence of nineteenth century studies, in addition to Ó Carragáin's (2005 & 2010) detailed work. The later medieval parish church is a structure with some architectural interest. Combined, these three churches provided valuable insights into the medieval Christian heritage of this part of Co. Mayo in terms of its history, archaeology and architecture.

Acknowledgements

Many thanks to Lynda Huxley and to Peter† and Pat Roberts of Kilkeeran who provided valuable assistance and insights while this research was being undertaken.

Bibliography

Printed primary sources

Anon. 1963. *Obligationes pro Annatis Diocesis Tuamensis. Archivium Hibernicium 26, 56-117.*

Egan, P.K. & Costello, M.A. 1958. *Obligationes pro Annatis Diocesis Clonfertensis. Archivium Hibernicium 21, 52-74.*

Egan, P.K. & Costello, M.A. 1958. *Obligationes pro Annatis Diocesis Clonfertensis. Archivium Hibernicium 21, 52-74.*

Giles, J.A. 1843. *The Ecclesiastical History of the English Nation Translated from the Latin of Venerable Bede. London, James Bohn.*

Stokes, W. 1905, (ed. and trans.). *The Martyrology of Óengus the Culdee. London, Harrison and Sons.*

Sweetman, H.S. & Handcock, G.F. 1896. *Calendar of Documents Relating to Ireland preserved in Her Majesty's Public Record Office London, 1302-1307. Dublin, A. Thom.*

Twemlow, J.A. (ed.) 1933. *Calendar of Entries in the Papal Registers Relating to Great Britain and Ireland, Papal Letters, Vol. XII AD 1458-1471. London, His Majesty's Stationery Office.*

Figure 11: *Interior view of the window in the southern wall of Ballyovey parish church.*

Figure 12: *East window of Ballyovey parish church.*

Secondary sources

Anon. 1861. General Alphabetical Index of Townlands and Towns, Parishes and Baronies in Ireland. Alexander Thom, Dublin.

Bhreathnach, E. 2014. Ireland in the Medieval World AD400-1000: Landscape, Kingship and Religion. Dublin, Four Courts Press.

Breen, A. 2009. Ciarán of Saighir. In J. McGuire and J. Quinn (eds) Dictionary of Irish Biography. Cambridge, Cambridge University Press.

Connolly, P. 2002. Medieval Record Sources (Maynooth Research Guides for Irish Local History). Dublin, Four Courts Press.

Downham, C. 2018. Medieval Ireland. Cambridge, Cambridge University Press.

Duffy, P.J. 2005. The shape of the parish. In E. FitzPatrick and R. Gillespie (eds) The Parish in Medieval and Early Modern Ireland. Dublin, Four Courts Press.

Farmer, D. 2004. Oxford Dictionary of Saints. Oxford, Oxford University Press.

Fawcett, R. 2002. Scottish Medieval Churches: Architecture and Furnishings. Gloucester, Tempus.

FitzPatrick, E. & Gillespie, R. (eds) 2005. The Parish in Medieval and Early Modern Ireland: Community, Territory and Building. Dublin, Four Courts Press.

FitzPatrick, E. 2005a. The material world of the parish. In E. FitzPatrick & R. Gillespie (eds) The Parish in Medieval and Early Modern Ireland: Community, Territory and Building, 62-75. Dublin, Four Courts Press.

Figure 13: *View towards the chancel of Ballyovey parish church with the east window in the centre.*

Herity, M. 2009. *Ordnance Survey Letters Mayo.* Dublin, Four Masters Press.

Huxley, C. & Huxley, L. 2015. *Lough Carra.* Castlebar, Co. Mayo, Carra Books.

Johnston, E. 2008. 'Munster, saints of'. *Oxford Dictionary of National Biography.* [Online] Hyperlink: https://doi.org/10.1093/ref:odnb/51008 (Accessed 29 July 2019).

Kinahan, G.H. 1868a. Cyclopean churches in the vicinity of Loughs Corrib, Mask and Carra, Part I. *Journal of the Historical and Archaeological Society of Ireland.* 1(1), 76-80.

Kinahan, G.H. 1868b. Cyclopean churches in the vicinity of Loughs Corrib, Mask and Carra, Part II. *Journal of the Historical and Archaeological Society of Ireland.* 1(1), 131-138.

Knox, H.T. 1904. *Notes on the Early History of the Dioceses of Tuam, Killala and Achonry.* Dublin, Hodges, Figgis and Co. Ltd.

Lavelle, D. 1994. *An Archaeological Survey of Ballinrobe and District, Including Lough Mask and Lough Carra.* NP, Lough Mask and Lough Carra Tourist Development Association.

Leask, H.G. 1955. *Irish Churches and Monastic Buildings (Volume I The First Phases and the Romanesque).* Dundalk, Dundalgan Press.

MacGabhann, F. 2014. *Logainmneacha Mhaigh Eo 5: Barúntacht Cheara.* Baile Átha Cliath, Coiscéim.

McNeill, T.E. 2006. *Faith, Pride and Works: Medieval Church Building.* Gloucestershire, Tempus.

Ní Ghabhláin, S. 1995. *Church and community in medieval Ireland: The diocese of Kilfenora.* JRSAI 125, 61-84.

Ní Ghabhláin, S. 1996. *The origin of medieval parishes in Gaelic Ireland: The diocese of Kilfenora.* JRSAI 126, 37-61.

Ó Carragáin, T. 2005. *Habitual masonry styles and the local organisation of church building in early medieval Ireland. Proceedings of the Royal Irish Academy.* 105C(3), 99-149.

Ó Carragáin, T. 2010. *Churches in Early Medieval Ireland: Architecture, Ritual and Memory.* London, Yale University Press.

Ó hÓgáin, D. 2006. *The Lore of Ireland: An Encyclopedia of Myth, Legend and Romance.* Woodbridge, Boydell Press.

O'Connell, J. & Costello, M.A. 1958. *Obligationes pro Annnatis Diocesis Ardfertensis. . Archivium Hibernicum 21,* 1-51.

OED, 2019. 'Cyclopean | Cyclopean, adj.' OED Online, Oxford University Press, [Online] Hyperlink https://oed.com/view/Entry/46546. Accessed 30 July 2019.

Stalley, R. 2005. *Ecclesiastical architecture before 1169. In D. Ó Cróinín (ed.) A New History of Ireland, Vol. I: Prehistoric and Early Ireland.* Oxford, Oxford University Press.

Stalsmans, N. & Charles-Edwards, T.M. 2007. *'Meath, saints of'. Oxford Dictionary of National Biography.* [Online] Hyperlink: https://doi.org/10.1093/ref:odnb/51010 (Accessed 29 July 2019).

Stevens Curl, J. 1999. *Oxford Dictionary of Architecture.* Oxford, Oxford University Press.

Dr Yvonne McDermott lectures on the History and Geography programme in GMIT Mayo Campus where she teaches archaeology and history modules. Her main research interest is the history, archaeology and architecture of the mendicant orders of friars in the west of Ireland in the late medieval period. She is a regular contributor to Cathair na Mart and other journals.

'PUTTING HER IN HER PLACE':[1]
WRITING NURSE EMILY MACMANUS INTO THE FACTUAL IRISH GREAT WAR RECORD

Alice McDermott

Throughout its hundred year aftermath, historians writing on the subject of the Great War generally agree that, conservatively estimating, somewhere in the region of four thousand five hundred[2] Irish nurses served, both on the home front and close to or on the front lines in all of its very many widely dispersed arenas of conflict, throughout the conflict that so unrestrainedly, persistently, and savagely raged for over four years between the years 1914 to 1918.

It is worth bearing in mind that those figures were subsequently and, indeed, continue to be, persistently 'cautiously guesstimated' for one very valid reason. It is this. Numbers were neither accurately nor comprehensively recorded as women were enlisting in the various professional and voluntary nursing services in 'real time,' in other words, as the Great War continued to thunder, rampage, and almost persistently wreak havoc.

Therefore, they were inevitably incorrect as they were being initially recorded throughout the inordinately long-time during which the conflict played out on its dismal, destructive, injurious, and, far too frequently, lethal 'fight path.' As noted, such inaccuracies were due to a combination of procedural error, especially unconcerned imprecision and absence of completeness while being detailed, a failure probably resulting, frankly, from a British statutory inability to recognise both their then and future significance and importance.

Whatever the full explanation for the consequently enduring erroneous calculation, it is definitely the case that the actual numbers of Irish nurses who ministered at home and overseas during the Great War was much higher than continues to be largely un-questionably accepted, possibly, even continuing to apply overly cautious approximations, at least double the quantity still so widely accepted as accurate.

While there might be lack of clarity and consequent small amounts of disagreements amongst interested parties about the exact amounts of Irish women who provided nursing service on home bases and abroad throughout the 1914 to 1918 conflict, what is clear and without doubt is that one such woman was Great War nursing veteran Emily Elvira Primrose MacManus.[3]

---

3 *Full name taken from the headstone of her grave located in St. Michael's Church of Ireland graveyard*

In the year marking the 100th anniversary of the ending of the 1914 to 1918 conflict, one of the bloodiest the world has ever seen,[4] Emily's inspiring Great War overseas nursing contribution is the focus of the current article. The reasons for making her war-work throughout that prolonged and appalling period the mainstay of the piece are twofold, firstly to facilitate her posthumously to take her hard-won and rightful place, together with all the male players, on the Irish part of the wretched Great War stage and, secondly, to pay tribute to her impressive input into the treatment and care of wounded and dying soldiers, padres, members of the medical teams, and civilians grievously impacted by the fifty one months of monstrous fighting.

This is Emily's Great War story
The eldest of five siblings,[5] she was born in London on 18 April 1886[6] to affluent and upper-class parents Leonard and Julia[7] MacManus.

England's capital city may have been the actual place of Emily's birth. It was also the dwelling place of the entire Mac Manus family for most of all of the years of the parents' and children's lives. However, interestingly, from a very early age and clearly influenced by her father's entirely apolitical attitude and outlook on 'national identity,' she and her two brothers and two sisters[8] regarded themselves as Irish, a position all the siblings were to steadfastly maintain for the remainder of their lives.[9]

The identification with the concept of Ireland being 'home' was profound within the five MacManus siblings, instilled as it was by their father from the outset of their individual and collective existences. Emily refers to the benevolent implanting of the notion in his children by her father at the beginning of her autobiography: '...Of one thing my father was determined; we were to be Irish children... He never let us forget that...That (standpoint) stamped Killeaden[10] (in county Mayo) as our family home on my memory for ever...'[11]

And so began a lifelong commitment and connection for Emily, her parents, and her siblings with the county and country to which they undoubtedly gave their

in Ballina, Co. Mayo.

4 *For some sense of this, see, for example, Ferguson, Niall, The Pity of War (Penguin Books, 1999).*

5 *Taken from her autobiography, MacManus, Emily, Matron of Guy's (Andrew Melrose, 1956), p. 7.*

6 *Birth date taken from Emily's headstone.*

7 *Nee Boyd.*

8 *See MacManus, Emily, Matron of Guy's, Op. Cit., p. 7. See, also, ouririshheritage.org/mayo people/ Emily Mac Manus.*

9 *For more information, see Rowley, Tom, Emily MacManus, Matron of Guy's: The Heroism of a Young Irish Nurse in Wartime Britain at womensmuseumofireland.ie.*

10 *The family home near Kiltimagh in Co. Mayo. For more details, see Ibid., p. 3.*

11 *From Ibid., p. 7*

foremost allegiances while simultaneously primarily living, growing-up, being educated, trained, and then working in England, the adopted country they loved and respected in almost equal measures.[12]

Not only that, the allegiance to and association with Ireland and Mayo was not merely ideological for the London based MacManus family. On the contrary, the 'connected' relationship with the place had very real substance for her parents, Emily, and her brothers and sisters. In other words, it was routinely practically applied as follows in all of their lives.

From her earliest years, Emily, together with her parents and siblings, spent time in Kileaden at least once per annum.[13] Of course these constant visits further copper fastened the sense of being Irish in the entire MacManus family. As Emily recalls in her book: '...Our best holidays were in Ireland...The journey was part of the adventure...(Upon arrival at Kileaden) there was always something going on, once an Irish historical play in the granary, written by Aunt Lottie[14]...Now and then there were dances (there)...I learned to draw turf...to stook oats, to manage a farm horse and cart...There were horses to ride...Aunt Emma used to arrange delicious expeditions for us and for the household...Best of all were those picnics to Lough Conn...'[15]

Consequently, and clearly intentionally for all of his children on her father's part, a permanent sense of belonging in and to Ireland and Mayo was fostered in the individual and collective hearts of the London established MacManus clan. This was to have powerful echoes and impacts for Emily and her siblings for the remainder of their lives, a pivotal circumstance for her and them that will be further discussed later.

After her schooling was complete, Emily choose to follow in the footsteps of two of her aunts and, of course, her father who was, by profession, a doctor,[16] by training to become a nurse.[17]

She commenced her three years training in nursing at Guy's hospital in London in May 1908. Having been deemed successful in same, she and those of her classmates who achieved equally fortunate results were declared fully trained nurses at the end of 1911.[18]

---

12 *For an indication of the depth of Emily's fondness and regard for London throughout the years of her growing up there, see, for example, Ibid., pp. 10-14.*
13 *For a brief account of the family's regular holidays in Mayo, see Ibid., pp. 17-21.*
14 *For more information on Emily's aunt, Charlotte MacManus, novelist and prominent member of the Irish Literary Revival, see kiltimagh.ie/lottie-charlotte-mac-manus.*
15 *Ibid., pp. 17-21.*
16 *See Ibid., p. 6 for further details relating to the professions of her aunts and father.*
17 *Ibid., pp. 31-32.*
18 *See Ibid., pp. 33-46 for more information on same.*

It was an apparently opportune time to graduate with a professional nursing quali-fication, the century was relatively new and seemingly promising, particularly for women who, since the 1870s, in ever increasing numbers, were beginning to come together and make very early calls for gender equality, principally through their lobbying for the right to vote, then-to-fore granted solely to men of economic and social status.[19]

What no one could have foreseen at the end of 1911 and the start of 1912, when Emily was basking in the joy of her (then) recent achievement, happily contem-plating her immediate future, and speculating that '…there was nothing (she) could not tackle…',[20] was that global war clouds were gathering that, once unleashed on the largely unsuspecting world, would play absolute havoc with its individuals, participating and otherwise, communities, places, infrastructures, governments, monarchies, militaries, economies, empires, political opinions, and social orders.[21]

Emily herself clearly didn't anticipate that what would happen (for the fifty one months between August 1914 and November 1918), to her and the entire world, could happen.

Instead, she, like everyone else, formed part of what has long been depicted by some historians and interested others as the globally inattentive masses suffering from a curiously numbing phenomenon that the recently published book titled, with a large measure of truth but nonetheless perhaps deeply unfairly, The Sleepwalkers,[22] and presents as an apparently worldwide state of heedlessness and stupefaction that, with the benefit of hindsight, appears extraordinarily brainless, particularly when it was universally shared, after all, how could everyone not have known what was go-ing to quickly transpire almost everywhere if they all kept doing and, perhaps more importantly, not doing, what they were then doing or failing to do?

Such an assessment is, of course, simultaneously conceived and incorrect.

That is simply because, in the moment, as governments and the military world-wide were saying certain things and related and other things were happening, they couldn't and, furthermore didn't see where it was all leading, and to expect them to without the assistance of retrospection is surely extremely partial and illogical, after all, causes and effects, sequences, consequences, etc. are only ever clear to those both directly involved and secondarily impacted after things have already happened, in other words, after events have taken their course.

---

19 *For an interesting assessment of female suffrage at this time, see, for example, Marlow, Joyce (Ed.), Votes for Women: The Virage Book of Suffragettes (Virago Press, 2001).*
20 *Mac Manus, Emily, Matron of Guy's, Op. Cit., p. 46.*
21 *See, for example, Ferguson, Niall, The Pity of War, Op. Cit.*
22 *Clark, Christopher, The Sleepwalkers: How Europe Went to War in 1914 (Penguin books, 2013).*

Be that as it may, in January 1912, Emily decided to augment her recently completed nursing training by starting a new course of instruction in midwifery at the East End Mothers' Home in London.[23] The programme there was informative and intensive but, regardless of the rigours consequently placed on her so soon after her initial nursing examinations, some four months later, by May1912, Emily had completed all theoretical and practical lessons, passed additional tests in same, and attained a second measure of nursing accreditation.

Armed with two sets of nursing qualifications, she began looking for relevant work experience and employment.

In this regard, the best prospect for a young, inexperienced nurse like Emily at the time was to register to provide 'holiday relief'[24] at home or abroad.

She did this and secured a temporary nursing post immediately. Interestingly, it was at a big hospital in Cairo in Egypt[25] which gave her a wonderful opportunity to travel, see the world, gain further proficiency in her chosen profession and, at the same time, earn money!

The Egyptian post lasted for approximately three months after which Emily returned to London.

Almost immediately, sometime in the late summer of 1912, she attained a second relief post, again of three months duration, this time in Guy's Hospital.[26] Intriguingly, and a measure of the regard in which she was held in the hospital where she had initially trained, she was selected for several further relief positions at Guy's.

When those came to an end, sometime in 1913, Emily was reliably informed by the (then) Matron that she had admirably impressed those with whom she had worked and would be chosen for a full sister's post at Guy's, probably sometime in the spring of 1914, when one next became available.[27]
Following some months of temporary nursing work at a hospital in Norfolk,[28] Emily was offered a permanent nursing position in Guy's in April 1914, four months prior to the outbreak of war.

Just over a year later, in July 1915, having already treated some Great War casualties, soldiers mainly, at her home front base hospital, Emily made the courageous

---

23 *Mac Manus, Emily, Matron of Guy's, Op. Cit., pp. 46 7.*
24 *See Ibid., p. 51.*
25 *See Ibid., pp. 51-72.*
26 *Ibid., p. 73.*
27 *Ibid., P. 78.*
28 *Ibid., pp. 79-83.*

and life altering determination to volunteer her nursing services overseas for the remainder of the conflict.

And it was an immensely brave decision. After all, as a fully qualified nurse who, by 1915, already had more than three years' work-experience where she had seen first-hand the physical and mental ravages and vulnerabilities of the human body, incorporating damage inflicted from all manner of things, including war (remember, the Boar War was then only twelve years concluded and she would have treated patients in London still permanently impaired as a result of having participated in same), and clearly familiar with surgical work and the traumas witnessed during same, she knew that she was, in a time of brutal war, most likely going to be assisting with surgeries necessitated by wounds incurred in battle and was, therefore, going to be exposed to and required to treat every manner and range of injury, from very minor to very major, and would have to cope with all the very many deaths that almost constant clashes inevitably implied, consciously and freely 'entering the gates of hell.'

Strikingly undeterred by the discomforts, heart-aches, worries, and dangers she was willingly embracing by volunteering to journey towards and work close to one of the very hearts of the conflict, Emily proceeded with her application to provide front-line nursing service throughout the Great War and was accepted into the (then) relatively newly established[29] but nonetheless hugely respected Queen Alexandra's Imperial Military Nursing Service[30] (Reserve), and despatched to the Western Front, to Etaples in France.[31]

From there, she was deployed with a team of professional and volunteer nurses to establish and then staff a field hospital, temporarily constructed entirely of tents, close to the village of Camiers[32] some four miles from Etaples and nearer to the front lines of the conflict.[33]

Fortunately for Emily, her nursing and doctor colleagues and, of course, wounded and dying patients, there was a more permanent medical treatment plan in place within the region. This was to build a solid hospital structure in Camiers from which war-time care could be given and received.

The hospital was duly constructed in the village of Camiers and it was there that Emily, specifically assigned to surgical work,[34] spent some of her time, close to the

---

29 *From Hallett, Christine, Containing Trauma: Nursing Work in the First World War (Manchester University Press, 2009), p. 7.*

30 *For an assessment of their status and reputation, prior to the Great War, see, for example, fairest-force.co.uk/The Fairest Force (QAIMNS) Before the War.*

31 *MacManus, Emily, Matron of Guy's, Op. Cit., pp. 89-90.*

32 *What was known as the 18th General in Camiers. See Ibid., p. 90.*

33 *Ibid., pp. 92-94.*

34 *Ibid., p. 96.*

front lines, throughout the Great War.

She and her nursing colleagues continued to sleep in tents at night however, a position that did not alter for the entire two and a half years she spent in the region. As a qualified nurse, she and her QAIMNS[35] colleagues, before, during, and after the very many surgical procedures they assisted with throughout the 1914 to 1918 conflict, while completing their own nursing tasks would also have undertaken the supervision and directing of the VADs[36] working alongside them in the wards and operating theatres of the hospital in Camiers.

Appealingly, (particularly for the writer of the current article who researches and documents, in the main, Irish Great War volunteer nurses for the simple reason that information about them is more readily available than for their professional counter-parts), Emily had great respect for the voluntary nurses she met and worked with in France throughout the Great War.

In a revealing comment about her own assessment of their value, early in the part of her account describing her experiences during the 1914 to 1918 conflict, about the generally less than flattering perceptions of them by Great War trained nurses and her own diametrically opposed positive response to them, she says of her unit's first time to work with them:

> '...Patients began to arrive at Camiers. At about the same time, we received our first contingent of V.A.D.s. This created consternation and annoyance among many of the regular Q.A. sisters in all the camps. "Army hospitals are not the place for untrained girls. They will be useless-frivolous, frightened." There was no end to the prophecies and forebodings...and the V.A.D.s were the greatest success.'[37]

Irrefutably due to Great War V.A.D.S the praise clearly was. It is, nonetheless, another pleasant sign of the type of person Emily was, fair, independent, and unthreatened by those outside her own professional remit.

For two and a half of the three years Emily spent serving overseas during the Great War, from July 1915 to January 1918, she remained on the surgical rota in the village hospital.

---

35 *The abbreviation by which the nursing outfit was most frequently denoted. For further details, see, for example, McEwan, Yvonne, In The Company Of Nurses: The History of the British Army Nursing Service in the Great War (Edinburgh University Press, 2014) and Piggott, Juliet, Queen Alexandra's Royal Army Nursing Corps (Leo Cooper Ltd., 1975).*
36 *The speedily and rudimentarily trained nurses working with the Voluntary Aid Detachment. For more information, see, for example, Dent, Olive, Volunteer Nurse on the Western Front (Ebury Publishing, 2014).*
37 *MacManus, Emily, Matron of Guy's, Op. Cit., pp. 94-95.*

Conditions specifically related to surgery throughout the conflict, indeed, every-where throughout the Great War, were hard, for nurses, doctors, and patients alike. The availability of equipment and medicine was never any better than mediocre and much more likely to be downright sparse.[38]

There was frequent pressure for space for patients and staff, in queueing areas for emergency and other procedures, in operating theatres, and in recovery wards, particularly at times when there were 'big pushes' in the fighting in any and all of the theatres of war.

And Emily's nursing duties, as noted, were expressly focused on the surgical front for most of her Great War overseas service in Camiers.[39]

She would therefore have been a part of various medical teams waiting in line for space in which to conduct often complex and life-threatening or saving operations, often in cramped spaces, with enormous pressures to conduct what unfortunately regularly became common-place procedures like amputations, on the one hand, and multi-faceted sutures to save body parts, on the other, more quickly, in greater numbers, to process the never ending queues of those awaiting treatment and care. All medical work, for both doctors and nurses, was routinely harrowing, pressur-ised, stressful, demanding, frequently distasteful, and downright heart-breaking throughout most of the entirety of the Great War.

They were, after all, dealing with a 'modern' war machine that was wreaking utter wreckage on the bodies and minds, sometimes both, of all those injured and dying as a result of the conflict.

As Lyn MacDonald, writing about the surgical work of doctors and, particular-ly, nurses throughout the Great War, so accurately, starkly, unambiguously, and poignantly stated:

> '...These (women) had to be tough. They worked in flooded operating thea-tres in Flanders where, in a big 'push,' there might be four operations going on at one time, and as many as ten amputations an hour.'

They nursed men with terrible wounds and (either) saw them off to convalescent camp or laid them out when they died.

---

38 *For accounts of the availability and otherwise of medical equipment, supplies, and limitations throughout the Great War, see, for example, Higonnet, Margaret, R. (Ed.), Nurses at the Front: Writing the Wounds of the Great War (Northeastern University Press, 2001); Hallett, Christine, Nurse Writers of the Great War (Manchester University Press, 2016); and MacDonald, Lyn, The Roses of No Man's Land (Penguin Books, 1993).*
39 *See MacManus, Emily, Matron of Guy's, Op. Cit., pp. 94-96, for additional details.*

They nursed in wards where the stench of gas-gangrenous wounds was almost overpowering.

They nursed men choking to death as the fluid rose in their gassed lungs , men whose faces were mutilated beyond recognition, whose bodies were mangled beyond repair, whose nerves were shattered beyond redemption...'[40]

This was the reality of Emily's life and work for the three years that she volunteered in France throughout the appalling conflict, a stark truth probably best served, particularly for the wounded and dying soldiers and their families most directly horrifically affected by what had befallen them as a result of combat, by leaving the adding of further details alone.

What she experienced and had to do while nursing in Camiers between 1915 and 1918 was undoubtedly regularly gruesome and traumatic for her. And yet, Emily never said any of that when describing her Great War nursing experiences in her autobiography.

This reveals another interesting, unsurprising, and agreeable aspect of her character and outlook, one that was, very often, shared by the hundreds of thousands of women, globally, who provided nursing care throughout the Great War.[41]

The only reason she wouldn't have divulged additional details about what she had seen and done while nursing in Camiers was that she had too much compassion and respect for all of the wounded soldiers and, perhaps, albeit to a much lesser extent, padres, members of the medical teams, and civilians in her care throughout her time close to the Western Front lines of the conflict to potentially add to their suffering by publishing details and descriptions about it. It is worth remembering that there were many Great War veterans, men and women, still alive when her book came out in 1956.

In the main, Emily witnessed a combination of horrific sights, sufferings, injuries, and deaths and, undoubtedly, joyous moments of full or partial recovery of patients and, of course, probably less frequent occasions of rest, leisure, during her time in France for three of the four years of the Great War.

---

40 *From MacDonald, Lyn, The Roses of No Man's Land (Penguin Books, 1993), p. xi. It is important to note that she was specifically referring to VADs. However, the qualified nurses were right beside the volunteer nurses in the Great War operating theatres. In fact, they did the bigger percentage of the surgical assistance because they were comprehensively qualified to do so. They also saw the same awful sights and smelled the same awful putrefying aromas.*
41 *To get a sense of how nurses who served at the front throughout the Great War and subsequently published their memories of same did not seek to sensationalise or overexpose the men and, to a lesser degree, women whom they treated, see, for example, Beauchamp, Pat, Fanny Goes to War (Meadow Books, 2005) and Cowen, Ruth (Ed.), War Diaries: A Nurse (Edith Appleton) at the Front (Simon & Schuster UK. Ltd., 2012).*

Some of the intense pressure and horror was removed from her, happily, for the last year of the Great War.

Sometime towards the end of 1917, probably because she had already spent an entire two and a half years working under the most stressful and extreme conditions possible for a professional Great War nurse, right at the heart of some of the surgical procedures that were such a simultaneously innovative and truly shocking inevitable consequence of 'modern' combat, particularly the damage to individuals caused by aerial bombardment, tanks, and poisonous gas,[42] Emily was assigned a less traumatic nursing position in the town of Dieppe approximately eighty miles away.

She and a group of professional nurses, with the assistance of four VADS, were asked to take over a former hotel on the beach in the town and transform it into a convalescent home for officers.[43]

Interestingly, upon first hearing of the new posting, she records in her autobiography one of her more 'telling' responses to three things, namely, her own commitment to war-time nursing care, her prior surgical work in Camiers, and the prevailing circumstances there for the past two and a half years with the following:
> '...A more complete contrast to our former job could not be imagined- a sunny sea-side town, a tourist hotel, striped bathing tents, good shops, a golf course; all working under limited wartime conditions, but still, there they were. After two years of flapping tents, down land and marsh, dust and mud, it seemed to me a comic change, and, strangely enough, not altogether to my liking...'[44]

The most interesting of the three observations, from the point of view of being given a further insight into the personality and outlook of Emily herself, in fact, the essence of her Great War contribution to nursing care in France, is the one regarding her essential dislike of her new working environment.

Her displeasure was clearly twofold. Firstly, used to considerably busier Great War work-loads and much happier to be occupied to that extent, she didn't really like the easier pace of her new working life. Nor did she like the less exacting demands of it.

However, much to her greater satisfaction, problems, pressures, and procedures soon piled up to fill the there-to-fore unwanted gaps in her work time and effort.45 The officers she and her medical colleagues looked after there were recovering

---

42 *For more information on same, see, for example, Westwell, Ian, The illustrated History of the Weapons of World War One (Southwater, 2011).*

43 *See MacManus, Emily, Matron of Guy's, Op. Cit., p. 100.*

44 *Ibid.*

45 *Ibid.*

from wounds ranging from minor to severe. As officers, they were also privy to more details about the course of Great War fighting on the Western Front and, while they would not have divulged details to members of the medical teams, it wouldn't have been difficult to ascertain that things were looking extremely dismal for the Allies with even the ultimate prospect of failure in the air.[46]

Around Christmas 1917, Emily was briefly posted, about forty miles away, to a hutted, in other words, a temporary hospital in the forest outside Rouen.[47]

In January 1918, she was despatched to a Casualty Clearing Station (No. 46) at Noyons approximately one hundred miles from Rouen.

Entirely in line with the type of person Emily appears to have been, practical, unafraid, hardworking, and anxious to get 'stuck-in' and make a significant contribution, she was extremely happy with this posting.

Writing about it some forty years afterwards, she described her response to being placed there with the following brief albeit revealing and fervent comment: '...I got my heart's desire...'[48]

At first, the work at the Casualty Clearing Station was relatively easy and unpressurised.

Then the Germans launched the Spring Offensive in March 1918 and 'all hell broke loose' for Allied military and medical personnel and all of those hapless civilians unfortunately caught up in the resultant carnage.[49]

In the hundred years since they wreaked their few months of total carnage and mayhem on their enemies, the 1918 German Spring Offensive has been comprehensively discussed and analysed by historians.
All are in general agreement as to the ferocious level and extent of the turmoil, chaos, dangers, discomforts, damages, injuries, and deaths visited on the allies by the intense German onslaught.

After all, it was big, bold, entirely unanticipated, constantly moving instead of relatively stationary (which had, until that point, been the trademark of all the Great War's battles) and, significantly, for approximately the first month of its operation, extraordinarily successful from a German perspective.[50]

46 See, for example, MacDonald, Lyn, They Called It Passchendaele (Penguin UK, 1993).
47 MacManus, Emily, Matron of Guy's, Op. Cit., p. 103.
48 Ibid., p. 106.
49 For details, see, for example, Gliddon, Gerald, Spring Offensive 1918 (Blackwell's, 2013).
50 For some accounts of the Kaiserschlacht, see, for example, Ferguson Niall, The Pity of War, Op. Cit.

For the first few days of the Spring Offensive, Emily's medical team stayed in place at the Casualty Clearing Station, desperately trying to treat the streams of wounded soldiers who were the unfortunate victims of the relentless German 'charge.'

As very quickly became the case with almost all Western Front allied soldiers, medical personnel, and civilians, wounded and otherwise, caught in the path of the German advance, remaining stationary ceased to be an option and so began a massive and rapid retreat by the Belgians, French, and British military and associated others from the intensity and severity of the German assault.

Emily's unit of medical staff and injured patients became part of this mass movement of allied soldiers and related others frantically fleeing back towards the French coast.

Her response to the Allied retreat is particularly revealing of her character and outlook.

Far from being frightened and cowed, Emily only describes feeling thoroughly 'sad (and) ashamed'[51] having to hastily evacuate the wounded and sundry others from the casualty clearing station and join the train of retreating allied soldiers, civilians, medical teams, and the wounded fleeing from the German onslaught.
Conditions while fleeing the enemy, for her, her colleagues and, of course, the wounded and dying in their care, were potentially mortally dangerous, stressful, unpleasant, frightening, extremely demanding, and exhausting.

And yet Emily never complained or expressed personal anxiety about that, reserving just two sentences in her memoir for how she actually felt when she witnessed, and very quickly realised the extent and severity of what was happening all around her, along with all the other members of the alliance against the central powers located on the Western Front, that an enormous and advancing offensive had been launched by the Germans. What she modestly recorded was this: '...And then the blow fell on March 21st, 1918...Soon it was very clear that something very serious was in progress...'[52]

They eventually joined a series of ambulance trains ultimately destined for Boulogne.[53]

For the remainder of the Great War, what has in recent times frequently been referred to as the last hundred days of the calamitous event, Emily served in a num-

and Stevenson, David, 1914-1918: The History of the First World War (Penguin Books, 2004).
51 See MacManus, Emily, Matron of Guy's, Op. Cit., p. 108.
52 Ibid., p. 106.
53 Ibid., p. 110.

ber of short-term posts, firstly, in a Casualty Clearing station at Longpre-le-Corps,[54] and from there, in very quick succession because the Allied medical teams were following the British, French, and Belgian rapid advances, from August 1918, in a camp outside Amiens,[55] then ones in Dernancourt,[56] Doignt near Peronne[57] and, finally, Bohain (en-Vermandois, in the region of Picardie).[58]

Bohain was to be Emily's last Great War overseas nursing posting because, happily, for her and the whole world, the armistice was signed on 11 November 1918 and the pointless, directionless, relentless, heartless conflict suddenly ceased.[59]

She did, however, serve briefly in one final overseas nursing post before returning home because, immediately the armistice was declared, she was transferred to a big base hospital at the port city of le Havre.[60]

As events transpired, she only worked there for a matter of days before receiving news that her mother was very ill and, on compassionate grounds, she was given special leave to return home. Her mother did make a full recovery from her illness but the unfortunate event resulted in Emily being given her discharge papers which meant that her Great War overseas nursing contract was terminated.[61]

And so ended Emily MacManus's Great War nursing contributions and experiences over a period of three years, from 1915 to 1918, in France.

That she herself had no idea of the enormity and gallantry of the part she played in Irish Great War nursing care on the Western Front is clear from the few short lines she penned in her autobiography about the England to which she returned in 1918.

With absolutely no reference to her own Great War overseas nursing inputs, proficiencies, and sacrifices, her only response to the end of this three year chapter in her life, a hugely significant one, in which she faced and coped with the wilful and varied destruction of the people in her care and the places in which she worked and lived, constant threats to her own and others' safety, life, rest, and relaxation, her thoughts were with other:

---

54 *Ibid., p. 112.*
55 *Ibid., p. 114.*
56 *Ibid., p. 115.*
57 *Ibid., p. 118.*
58 *Ibid., p. 120.*
59 *For a recent account of the ending of the Great war, see, for example, Lloyd, Nick, Hundred Days: The Campaign That Ended World War One (Penguin Books, 2014).*
60 *From MacManus, Emily, Matron of Guy's, Op. Cit., p. 121.*
61 *Ibid., p. 121-122.*

'...I found an austere, exhausted, and short tempered England (and) began to realise that, in war, those who are left behind have as hard a time...as those who go out to fight (and save lives)...'[62]

Those words, the last she uttered in her memoir about her Great War nursing undertakings in France, are suitable ones with which to conclude this exploration of her war-work on the Western Front from 1915 to 1918 because they clearly illustrate her self-effacing disregard for all that she risked (especially her own personal safety) and endured over a three year period in her attempts to relieve the suffering of those wounded and dying, including military and medical personnel and civilians, as a direct result of the fighting.

Those assertions, in fact, together with her conduct and demeanour throughout the approximately thirty six months (three of the four years of the 1914 to 1918 conflict) during which she served as a member of the QAIMNS team of nurses on the Western Front are the distinct hallmarks of a Great War heroine whose courage and selfless care to the wounded and dying, almost always under conditions of 'fire,' deserves to be remembered and honoured in Ireland for as long as there are citizens to do just that!

For the purposes of completion, there are three points of information regarding Emily's post- Great War worthy of brief final note.

Firstly, she became assistant matron of Guy's hospital soon after her return from Great War nursing service abroad[63] and matron in 1927.[64] She held the matron's post for almost twenty years.

Secondly, upon her retirement from the position in 1946,[65] Emily returned to Pontoon in County Mayo, close to where her family home had been, and spent the next twenty two years, the remainder of her life, there.[66]

Thirdly, aged almost ninety two, she died in 1978 and is buried in the cemetery of St. Michael's Church of Ireland in Ballina where her tombstone captures some of the remarkable highlights of her extraordinary life. [67]

---

62 *Ibid., p. 122.*
63 *Ibid., pp. 123-124.*
64 *Ibid., p. 141.*
65 *See kiltimagh.ie/Emily-McManus.*
66 *Ibid.*
67 *The author has visited and photographed Emily's final resting place.*

Alice McDermott is a (Retired) Lecturer in History and Cultural Studies from Waterford Institute of Technology. She holds an M.A. in History from U.C.G. and an M.A. in History and Local Studies from U.L .She has published over forty articles on the Redmond family (John, William, and Bridget) political tenures, impact, and legacy in Waterford; Charles Bianconi; South East of Ireland Great War nurses Molly O'Connell Bianconi, Venice Hackett, Violet O'Neill Power, Lady Dorothie Fielding, and Kathleen Murphy; South East of Ireland Great War soldiers Captain Gerald Fitzgerald, Captain Learo Hackett, Second Lieutenant Eric Hackett, Private John Daly, Major William Redmond, and Lt. Col. Alfred Murphy; and a small number of Great War soldiers and nurses from the West of Ireland. Originally from Galway and with relatives in Easkey, Co. Sligo, she has always known about and been fascinated by the life of Emily MacManus.
amcdermott@wit.ie

WARTIME EVENING

by Ger Reidy

Late for the five o clock
He whipped the mare towards the station.
Standing alone in the cart legs splayed,
With parcels for the factory, Paul Henry
Cumuli towering behind him in the May sunshine.

Rope tied around the topcoat, two teeth in his head,
My aunt collected the dung off the cobbles,
Dev's tariff keeping the girls at the mill,
The thread broke but nobody complained,
Memories of the black and tans still raw.

When a U boat scuttled a warship they cheered.
Vertical turf smoke in the valley
Hoof echo under the bridge
The train engine idling in the new heat
At the mercy of Josie and the Clydesdale.

FRIENDS OF THE CLEW BAY
HERITAGE CENTRE

Noelene Crowe, Castlebar.

Anne Duffy, Westport.

Gerardine Cusack, Dublin.

Fiona MacBride, New Zealand.

Charlie Keating, Westport.

Seamus O'Connell, Westport.

Dr Oliver Whyte, Westport.

Eugene McCann, Newry.

Michael Moran, Limerick.

Margaret Ann Nuttall, Lancashire.

Suzette Hughes, Lankill, Westport.

Michael Kelly, Dublin.

Anna May McCreave, Westport.

Paul Smith, Foxford.

Patsy Gibbons, Westport.

Patrick McGinley, Galway.

Dympna Joyce, Castlebar.

Pauline Ford, Essex, England.

Noreen Sadler, Westport.

McLoughlin's Bookshop, Westport.

Paul Keogh, Dublin 6.

Robert Scott, Rare & Recent Books, Cong.

Joe McGovern, Newport.

Shirley Piggins, Westport.

Michael McDonnell, Australia.

Declan Dever, Westport.

June Bourke, Westport.

Liamy McNally, Sheeaune, Westport.

Milo Spillane, Co. Limerick.

Michael McGinley, Dublin.

Jennifer Waldron Lynch, Co Meath

Dr John Bradley, Murrisk, Westport.

Michael O'Sullivan, Westport.

Michael O'Donnell, Westport.

John and Merci Staunton, Westport.

Maire Nic an Fhailghigh, Castlebar,.

Seamus Duffy, Bookshop, Westport.

Ger Reidy, Westport.

Eleanor deEyto, Newport.

Mary Grady, Westport.

Martin Brady, Westport.

John J. Madigan, Westport.

Patrick Durcan, Westport.

Michael Rabbett, Westport.

Maureen Fitzsimons, Westport.

Sean Cadden, Westport.

Seamus Duffy Bookshop, Westport.

Harry Hughes, Westport.

Anne Duffy, Athlone.

John Shanley, Westport.

Prof. Cormac O'Malley, Dublin.

Helen & Peter Shanley, Westport.

Emer Cadden, Westport.

Anthony Jordan, Dublin.

Julia Thomas, New Zealand.

John O'Callaghan, Ennis.

Gerard Doherty, Dublin.

Christy Irwin, Westport.

Dr. Tim McDonnell, Dublin.

Michael Fitzgerald, P.A. USA.

Michael Casey, New Jersey, USA.

Anne Doherty, Westport

Éamon De Búrca, Blackrock, Dublin.

Fr Karl Burns, Mountbellew.

Tomas Ó Ceallaigh, Béal Asa.

Art Lavelle, Pershore, England.

Dr. Seán Lysaght, Westport.

McLoughlin's Bookshop, Westport.

Pat Bree, Westport.

We regret that two of our faithful friends and supporters *Mary O'Mahony*, Cross, and *Liam Lyons*, Westport, have passed on since our last Journal. We extend our deepest condolences to their families.

If you wish to support Clew Bay Heritage Centre and Westport Historical Society please become a Friend. Annual Subscription is €30. In return you get a free copy of any of our publications and 10% discount on genealogical research.